NOTES FROM THE FLAGSHIP

Thirty Leadership Lessons
from a Pastor and Para-Church Leader

DON WILKERSON

CONTENTS

INTRODUCTION

This manuscript started out as teaching material only for leaders in Teen Challenge, of which there are 1,400 centers in more than 125 countries. As I write this, I am back for the second time as leader of the first and original Teen Challenge, often referred to as the "Flagship" Center, thus the name, *Notes from the Flagship.*

These blog-type writings are not sent to all the Teen Challenge worldwide leaders, as many do not speak English; but a large number of leaders and staff receive my monthly writings. The feedback has been so positive I decided to expand it to include addressing issues that hopefully relate to pastors, as well as para-church leaders, whether the latter are in Teen Challenge or in other organizations. I have spent over fifty years as a para-church leader and around ten years as a pastor of two churches (one very small and the other, Times Square Church, very large). These ministry experiences have spanned over five decades. In addition, I grew up in a pastor's home and I am the third generation of ministers in the Wilkerson lineage.

I am privileged to be the co-founder of Brooklyn Teen Challenge with my brother David, serving twenty-six years in various capacities, ending up as Executive Director when my brother went on to do crusade evangelism under the umbrella of World Challenge. In 1987 it was my privilege again to partner with my brother in the founding of Times Square Church. My nearly eight years there was surely one of the highlights of all my years in ministry. In 1995, I resigned from Times Square Church and founded Global Teen Challenge, helping to plant the ministry around the world.

I retired in 2007, looking forward to writing, itinerate preaching and other things retirees do. I didn't have much of a chance to find out all that retirees do, because in 2008 I was asked by the Brooklyn Teen Challenge board to recommend someone as Executive Director. I recommended myself! I'm now in my eleventh year of my one-year commitment to Brooklyn Teen Challenge. My time is spent mainly in Brooklyn, but my home is actually in Virginia, although I don't get there too often. From my ministry assignments, I have years of experience to draw upon. Someone may ask, "How do you get experience?" The answer is to make a lot of mistakes. That I have done. Experience is a good teacher, both from failures and successes. Hopefully, I will ultimately be remembered for having more of the latter than the former.

Many of the subjects addressed are familiar to leaders, but I hope to provide new insights. An entire book could be written on some of the following articles, but I have chosen to keep them short, touching upon a number of leadership topics. In certain cases, I write what I have learned, both from the writings of other authors and from my experiences. I'm indebted to my mentors, both dead and alive. My pastor father and mother helped shape my early Christian life, as well as my preparation for ministry. My brother David has been my mentor in more ways than he ever knew. I miss him very much! The writings and lives of men such as Oswald Chambers, A. W. Tozer, Charles Spurgeon and contemporaries such as Billy Graham, John Maxwell, Charles Swindoll, and John Piper have impacted my ministry and spiritual life.

I have led both large and small numbers of staff and volunteers, as well as having been a pastor and leader to thousands of men, women and youth with serious, life-controlling problems. Working in Teen Challenge in many ways is similar to those of most pastors. However, leading a ministry that is operating 24/7 has given me an opportunity to apply biblical principles in ways that I could never have done so in a traditional pastoral ministry. Prayerfully, these principles are reflected in *Notes from the Flagship.*

Don Wilkerson, President
Brooklyn Teen Challenge

PART ONE
Inspiration and Instruction

1

THE SLOTHFULNESS OF BUSYNESS

*On the seventh day God had finished
his work of creation, so He rested
from all his work* (Genesis 2:2).

Slothfulness (laziness) and being busy seem to be a contradiction of terms. They are in the natural, but not in the spiritual realm.

I know how to keep busy in order to avoid doing things I don't enjoy. For instance, I'd actually rather get a root canal than do my taxes. I will keep busy at certain things to avoid getting administrative and other ministry things done. Worst of all, I can bury myself in sermon preparation, writing, and Bible study as a substitute for spending time in prayer. I call this *the slothfulness of busyness.*

There is a laziness of the body and mind, but there is also a laziness of the soul and spirit. It takes a greater discipline for some to be quiet than to be active. Waiting on God like a waiter or waitress in a restaurant (working for Him) is much easier for most Christians than waiting before Him (in quiet).

Peter challenged women (and men as well, but primarily women) to not be so concerned about their outward appearance, but to cultivate the inner person. *"You should be known for the beauty that comes from within, the unfading beauty of a gentle and quiet spirit, which is so precious"* (1 Peter 3:4). My wife spends the typical time a woman needs to get dressed and prettied for the day, but her time with the Word and prayer always comes first. On those days when we get up early for church or other activities, she rises earlier, so as not to miss her devotional time.

Unfortunately, the church as a whole is good at substituting program activities for prayer, worship and the Word. One can get addicted to *doing* at the expense of *being* in the presence of God. *"Cloaked by over activity, a typical day in the life of many of us is marked with avoidance and escape"* (Phileena Heuertz).[1] Because I am a person of action, doing, planning—things that others might commend me for—this can become my Achilles' heel. "Good" can be the enemy of "the best." Andy Stanley says, *"Being busy isn't the same as being productive."*[2] There can be a laziness of the spirit in feeding the spirit. We come to Christ by faith and not by works (See Ephesians 2:9), but we can get caught up in "works" to avoid other important matters in our walk of faith.

Mary and Martha of Bethany were greatly loved by Jesus. If He had any headquarters near Jerusalem, it was their home. The two sisters give us the contrast between serving Jesus and having intimate fellowship with Him. When Martha said to the Lord that it was unfair for Mary to sit and listen to Him while she prepared a big dinner (Luke 10:38-40), Jesus responded that Mary had chosen the *"better part"* of serving Him (Luke 10:41-42, KJV). Jesus was not making a comparison, but a contrast. He was not putting down what Martha was doing, but He was lifting up what Mary was doing at that moment, as a priority. Dinner can wait when the opportunity of being in His presence is available.

I find Martha and Mary acting in character upon the death of Lazarus. Jesus finally came on the scene after Lazarus was already buried, and Martha went out to meet Him. We don't know for sure, but it seems she gave Him a mild rebuke. *"Martha said to Jesus,*

'Lord, if you had been here, my brother would not have died'" (John 11:21).

Mary did not go out to meet Jesus. She stayed at home (See John 11:20). I picture Martha rushing to meet Jesus, standing, waiting for Him and the other disciples to approach the house with her hands on her hips, ready to give Jesus a rebuke for not being in a hurry to help. Mary, however, was being Mary; sitting, waiting, not for a miracle, but anticipating fellowship with the One she loved. Who did Jesus ask for as soon as He came near the house? Mary. She was called aside from the mourners because Jesus wanted to see her. She said the same thing as Martha, that if He had been there, her brother would not have died. Here's the difference between the two sisters: *"When Mary arrived* [outside their house] *and saw Jesus, she fell at His feet"* (11:32). I see Martha as the constant worker, and Mary as the consistent worshipper.

We need both Marthas and Marys in the body of Christ. We are prone, however, to be more of a Martha than a Mary. J. C. Ryle wrote, *"The restless, high-pressure hurry in which men live their lives endangers the very foundations of personal religion."*[3] Brother Lawrence, who apparently had the luxury of living in a time and era when life was not so hectic, said, *"Our only business is to love and delight ourselves in God."*[4] It is possible to do the things necessary at work, home and church while we delight in God, but it takes a strong daily commitment to not practice the "slothfulness of busyness."

Proverbs 24 describes a lazy person who lets his vineyard grow over with weeds and allows the walls to be broken down. From this we can learn a lesson: *"A little extra sleep, a little more slumber, a folding of the hands to rest—and poverty will pounce on you like a bandit; scarcity will attack you like an armed robber"* (30-34). The "slothful busy person" would never allow this to happen. He or she would pull up the weeds and never allow thorns to grow. However, while giving so much attention to the vineyard, this same industrious worker might come to spiritual poverty and be robbed of a relationship with the very Creator of that same vineyard.

> *God will never adjust His agenda to fit ours. He will not speed up His pace to catch up with ours; we need to slow our pace in order to recover our walk with Him. God will not scream and shout over the noisy clamor. He expects us to seek quietness, where His still small voice can be heard again* (Charles Swindoll).[5]

The Psalmist said he did not try to figure out matters too great for him. Instead, he writes: *"But I have stilled and quieted myself, just as a small child is quiet with its mother. Yes, like a small child is my soul within me"* (Psalm 131:1). The soul, like the body, lives on what it is fed.

Leaders, if we do not come apart and rest awhile, we will come apart in a little while! A person who does not know how to discipline himself to take "down time" may be active, but he or she will not be as productive. Everyone, especially those who are busiest, needs to be led by *"quiet waters"* (Psalm 23:2). That is where we will find much needed refreshment and restoration for our souls.

02/ 14 / 2023

2
FRONT SLIDING

*It is fine to be zealous, providing the
purpose is good* (Galatians 4:18).

A brother in Christ picked me up one Sunday morning so I could speak in his church. He was a lay person. Our conversation led to a discussion about the end times and Bible prophecy. After hearing him share very passionately about his views on the subject, I said to him, "I think you should be careful about such things, because if the devil can't get you to backslide, he'll get you to front slide."

He got very quiet for a moment and then said, "I've never heard of front sliding. Can you tell me what that is?"

I prayed silently and asked the Holy Spirit to tell me what it meant, because I never used that word before! It was one of those times when what came out of my mouth had not been in my spiritual knowledge bank. I paused some moments, waiting for the interpretation from God.

"Front sliding is when you study one truth and neglect other truths; you become unbalanced in your spiritual walk. It's kind of like eating only meat, and no vegetables."

The brother remained silent for the rest of the drive to church. I could tell he was trying to digest my answer, and I wondered if I had said the right thing to him.

As soon as I arrived at the church, I explained to the pastor what I had said to this gentleman so that he could either confirm or retract what I shared.

The pastor smiled and said, "Oh, Brother Wilkerson, that was a word from the Lord to that man. He's a former hippie who got wonderfully saved and was a great witness for the Gospel. Then he got caught up in reading and studying everything he could get his hands on about the last days. He bought a farm and now all he does is read the news and try to interpret it with all the teachings of Jesus, Daniel and Revelation on the end times. He has become an end-time 'sign-chaser.'"

One can front slide into many biblical truths like this former hippie. The greatest example is the "law and circumcision followers" of the New Testament. Galatians was written to these front sliders. In Galatians, Paul uses strong language when he says, *"You are already following a different way that pretends to be the Good News but is not the Good News at all. You are being fooled by those who twist and change the truth concerning Christ. Let God's curse fall on anyone, including myself, who preaches any other message than the one we told you about"* (Galatians 1:6-8).

Ways to Front Slide

I will leave it up to the reader to identify all the different ways one can front slide. However, a few examples of my own are in order:

- Evangelism without discipleship results in decisions for Christ without disciples of Christ.
- A church or ministry committed to helping converts to become strong disciples can neglect reaching the lost.

- Preaching grace without obedience can lead to what some have called *cheap grace,* leading to a compromising lifestyle lacking holiness.
- A church or ministry that focuses on a single social issue (abortion, politics, racism, etc.) to the neglect of other truths and issues, can be unaware of its own front sliding.
- Holiness teaching can become legalistic if not balanced with grace.
- Elevating one spiritual gift above others can lead to self-righteousness, pride, and front sliding.

I will never forget a statement from one of my college professors and how it applies to the concept of front sliding: "All Word, and we dry up. All Spirit, and we blow up. Word and Spirit together, we grow up!"

The book of Galatians deals with Jewish believers sliding forward (some might also call it backward) into the law again. These newborn believers were not going back to the world, but were sliding forward into their old way of trying to please God, thinking that through the observation of the law and circumcision they obtained salvation. Paul called such a belief foolish (See Galatians 3:1).

Paul said they were running a good race, but they then ran down the path of works, rather than faith. We see the same today—those who live by certain do's and don'ts not commanded in Scripture. By doing so, they do in principle what the church in Galatia did. They front slide! Beware of front sliders, as well as backsliders. In both cases, the result is often a deception of the enemy!

Paul questioned these Galatians about their turning back to the law as the basis of their salvation: *"You were running a good race. Who cut in on you and kept you from obeying the truth?"* (Galatians 5:7) This question may be applied to other front sliders. In Galatians, chapter three, verse five, Paul asks, *"Who has bewitched you?"*

Rightly Dividing the Truth

For centuries, churches have been divided by the overemphasis of one biblical truth at the expense of others. Some Christians have ended up being useless to the church because they took a truth and turned it into the whole Gospel. The greatest error of doctrine and truth is when a part becomes the whole!

New believers are especially subject to becoming overzealous with certain truths, such as soul- winning, holiness teaching, Holy Spirit empowerment, or the gifts of the Spirit. The church that offers good discipleship classes can avoid such pitfalls.

A. W. Tozer writes: *"The church must examine herself constantly to see if she is in the faith; she must engage in severe self-criticism with a cheerful readiness to make amends; she must live in a state of perpetual penitence, seeking God with her whole heart; she must constantly check her life and conduct against the Holy Scriptures and bring her life into line with the will of God."*[1]

Paul admonished Timothy, *"Be diligent to present yourself approved to God, a worker who does not need to be ashamed, rightly dividing the word of truth"* (2 Timothy 2:15, NKJV). The *"rightly dividing"* is from a single Greek word *orthotomero* meaning "straight cut; that is to rightly deal with a thing." Paul's best word on this is 2 Timothy 3:16, *"**All Scripture** (author's emphasis) is God-breathed and useful for teaching, rebuking, correcting and training in righteousness, so that the man of God may be* *thoroughly equipped for every good work"* (NIV). If some part of the Scripture is not taught and emphasized, the worker is only partially equipped, and not *"thoroughly equipped"* to do the work of God.

3

HOW TO STAY FAITHFUL
IN A THANKLESS ENVIRONMENT

*Endure suffering along with me
as a good soldier of Jesus Christ*
(2 Timothy 2:3).

I have been fortunate to have served most of my ministry in environments where my service was appreciated. There was one exception, so I know firsthand the challenge of what author Damian Kyle shares in a small booklet entitled, *Unappreciated— Serving God in a Thankless Environment.* Kyle uses the Apostle Paul as an example. I can identify on some level when Paul writes, *"At my first defense, no one came to my support"* (2 Timothy 4:16). The King James Version says, *"No man stood with me."*

My pastor father wrote in his diary many years ago how various church board members stood against him on issues in the church. On one occasion things came to a head on a Sunday morning when he had invited a pastor friend to come and speak. The evening before, there had been a heated board meeting. It didn't go well, at least not for my father. He went to the morning service still seething from the night before. He walked to the pulpit and said, "I resign," and then remarked to his friend, "Come on. Let's get out of here." My father left that church on the spot and never returned!

Dad was able to laugh about it later and realize that his youthful zeal and anger got the best of him. By the time I was born, my father had served for some years in three different churches, and was loved and appreciated by those congregations. I learned from him how to handle tough board issues.

One of the greatest challenges to pastors and leaders is to serve in places with people who lack simple appreciation and are unsupportive. Gratitude is an attitude, and ingratitude is also an attitude.

Paul's Thankless World

No one except for Jesus served in a more thankless environment than the Apostle Paul. Because of my own experience, I am deeply moved when he writes, *"I will very gladly spend and be spent for your souls; though the more abundantly I love you, the less I am loved"* (2 Corinthians 12:15, NKJV).

The church at Corinth gave Paul headaches and heartaches. He was loved by some and disliked by others. Some felt he was too simple, not flashy enough in his preaching style. Worst of all, some felt he was overly intolerant of their sinful behavior and carnality. From the two letters to the church at Corinth, Paul shares five things that can be helpful to anyone serving faithfully in a church where certain factions do not show the gratefulness they should.

1. Don't be swayed by the opinion of the minority.

In 1 Corinthians 4:1, Paul said he cared *"...very little if I am judged by you or by any human court."* In the court of human or church opinion, Paul paid little attention to their verdict of him. He did not mean this applied to everything they thought about him, but it definitely applied to the issues of their harsh judgments of him. Leaders cannot expect to be loved at all times and by everyone, but when we feel we have the mind of the Lord and a clear direction from

His Word, then human opinion should not keep us from faithful service.

Paul was open to listen to criticism, but he did not allow it to get him down or to persuade him away from the truth. As Damian Kyle wrote, *"There are times when we are tempted to give undue weight to the assessment of that small group in the church with the critical spirit, but to do that can drive us right out of the place that God has called us to serve Him."*[1]

2. Beware of too much self-judgment!

I saw my father go through too much worrying about the opinions of certain board and church members. When he took the issues to the Lord and felt he had the mind of God, he did as the Apostle Paul, who said, *"I do not even judge myself"* (1 Corinthians 4:1). In other words, Paul is saying, "Do not pass judgment on yourself." Kyle goes on to write:

> *For some of us, by virtue of our personalities, the greatest danger to remaining faithful in the place that God has called us is the opinions of others. But for others among us, the critic that lives within and the impossible standard that we established for ourselves is our great danger. The apostle Paul recognized that giving undue weight to his own judgment of himself was as dangerous and destructive as giving undue weight to the judgment of others. We have to recognize that introspection and self-examination can diminish our effectiveness, fruitfulness, and*

longevity as easily as criticism can.

I couldn't agree more completely. I am still prone to second guess myself after making decisions. Even after preaching a sermon, I might wonder, "Did it go over as well as I wanted? Did I leave some important truth out? Was it over people's heads?" As I grow older, I do less criticism and second-guessing of myself than I used to. Too little self-examination is not good, but too much self-judgment is not good, either. I have tried to remember this saying: *"Always accept criticism, but never accept judgment"* (James Richards).[2]

3. When proceeding in the face of opposition, have a clear conscience.

There needs to be discernment as to whether opposition is God-sent or man-motivated. My mother once shared something important with me when my brother David and I were at the height of establishing the Teen Challenge ministry. As we were riding the crest of ministry success, she said, "I pray you boys out of more things than I pray you into things." Then she explained her reasoning: "I see people coming to you with all kinds of ideas, projects and requests— but you can't do everything." Sometimes positive support can push us into things that are not what God wants, not best for us or the ministry.

When we do go down a road we are not certain of and someone questions us, we need to weigh whether it is God speaking through the questioner. However, when we are sure of the path we've chosen and we stand up for the principles and the direction we have chosen, a clear conscience enables us to have peace even when contrary winds blow our way.

Sometimes a clear conscience needs to be maintained when a door is unexpectedly closed in our face, and we have to move on to another place of service. I faced such a challenge. After founding a ministry and serving in it faithfully for many years, I decided it was time to step down. A short time later, I reconsidered and asked the board of directors to allow me to stay on for one more year of service. A staff member had suggested I stay the additional year to celebrate a special anniversary of the ministry. However, several board members opposed my request for the year extension. It was a hard pill to swallow. I knew my motives were pure, so I accepted it with a clear conscience and retired, or so I thought.

To be fair to the members of that board (most who were and still are friends of mine) there were other issues involved for which they opposed my desire to remain another year. Our differences were amicable. In the providence of God, it turned out that the Lord had another assignment waiting for me that I did not know at the time, that is, returning to the very ministry for which I was co-founder—Brooklyn Teen Challenge. I went from what could have been a perceived unfriendly environment to the friendliest and most appreciative environment I have ever served in. Now I can say I see the hand of God in the decision a board made to prevent me from serving another year in that ministry. During all this it was important that no root of bitterness spring up in me, and that I maintain a clear and clean conscience. Paul writes in 2 Corinthians 1:12, *"Now this is our boast: Our conscience testifies that we have conducted ourselves in the world, and especially in our relations with you, in the holiness and sincerity that are from God. We have done so not according to worldly wisdom, but according to God's grace."*

4. We ultimately will be judged by an audience of One!

"It is the Lord who judges me" (1 Corinthians 4:4). When it's all been said and done, we have to give an account of ourselves and our reputation to the Lord, whom we serve before and above all others. I once heard Greg Laurie share, *"If you take care of your character, God will take care of your reputation."* Unfortunately, sometimes it takes months or years before others see that their opposition to a pastor or leader was wrong, but more often such persons never see their wrong. Even Paul said some things will not be rightly judged *"...till the Lord comes"* (1 Corinthians 4:5, NIV).

A friend's son is the pastor of a church where a small group tried to maintain control and found fault with every pastor who came to serve. Finally, when they accused my friend's son of financial misbehavior, he stood up to them. His denomination exonerated him, and he remained there even though that faction of the church continued to be hostile toward him. When they realized they could not remove the pastor, the complainers all left. Now, new people are coming to fellowship there, but it took years to break the controlling spirits in that church. This pastor maintained his godly character throughout the years, always looking out upon the congregation knowing a divisive group was in attendance week after week. Often criticism says more about the critics than the one being criticized.

5. Faithfulness should have no shadow of turning.

James' Epistle says that all gifts come from the Father above *"...with whom is no variableness, neither shadow of turning"* (1:17). The faithful servants do not allow the opinions, criticisms, challenges and unfriendly environments to cause them to run away. They stand! They stay put! Paul said this is required of faithful stewards: *"Now it is required that those who have been given a trust must prove faithful"* (1 Cor. 4:2, NIV). A faithful steward does not turn with every wind of opposition and become what others want the leader to be, but instead remains steadfast.

Finally, Damian Kyle writes to the unappreciated:

> *Faithfulness in Him keeps us in the place of service. Paul realized that as difficult as Corinth was for him, God had called him to serve there, and as miserable as the circumstances were in many respects, he would continue to serve. Maybe you need to freshly commit to the place where God has called you to be—in that one-sided marriage; with that ungrateful child; in that thankless job or ministry. Whatever it might be, do it as an expression of worship to the Lord.*[3]

> *So, my dear brothers and sisters, be strong and steady, always enthusiastic about the Lord's work, for you know that nothing you do for the Lord is ever useless* (1 Corinthians 15:58).

4

WHAT CAN ELDAD AND MEDAD
TEACH US TODAY?

But Moses said, "I wish that all the Lord's
people were prophets, and that the Lord
would put His Spirit on them"
(Numbers 11:29).

In the book of Numbers, chapter 11, we read the story of two brothers, Eldad and Medad. They are not well-known Bible characters, but they have much to teach those in ministry about what happens when there is jealousy and a controlling spirit towards other ministers, ministries, churches and movements.

Moses was complaining to God that the Israelites were too many people for him to handle. God's response was immediate. The Lord spoke to Moses and said, *"Is there any limit to My power?"* (Numbers 11:23) Moses was limiting God's power to take care of the people under his care. He could not see that others could be anointed to serve. Then, in obedience to the Lord's instructions, Moses gathered seventy elders/leaders from the people and stationed them at the Tabernacle to assist him in meeting the needs of the congregation. As a result, an amazing thing happened! *"And the Lord came down in a cloud and spoke to Moses. He took some of the Spirit that was upon Moses and put it on the seventy leaders. They prophesied as the Spirit rested on them"* (Numbers 11:25).

Two of the seventy men were not at the Tabernacle when this happened—Eldad and Medad. Nevertheless, they had the Spirit of prophecy rest on them as well. *"They were listed among the leaders but had not gone out to the Tabernacle, so they prophesied there in the camp"* (11:26). How dare they? These two brothers were outside the camp prophesying and Joshua complained to Moses about it. This is recorded in Numbers 11:23-30.

A young man—probably the local gossip—ran to Moses and complained that these two men were out of order. Even Joshua, the Assistant Pastor, protested, saying to Moses, *"My master, make them stop"* (11:28).

Unfortunately, I see this type of behavior all the time. One person is used of the Lord in a way that is different from the normal order of things and another person steps in and tries to stop them. It occurs in local churches when department heads in the church try to control every aspect of their area of ministry. Or, God raises someone up with a gift in leadership and because of jealousy, they are hindered rather than allowed to be used in their gifting.

Pastors/leaders need to guard against such a move to stop what God wants to do in the church. Even a godly leader like Joshua can unwisely try to shut down the operation of a gift or gifts of the Spirit. Mission leaders and missionaries on the field can try to exercise territorialism and stop another group from coming into what they consider their ministry domain.

I always try to be aware of my own spiritual blindness in this regard. The flesh wants to control, but the Spirit wants to unleash power on other ministers, ministries, organizations and churches.

Jesus' disciples did the same thing in the New Testament. They came to Him saying, *"Teacher, we saw a man using your name to cast out demons, but we told him to stop because he wasn't one of our group"* (Mark 9:38). How did both Moses and Jesus react? Moses said, Give me more men like Eldad and Medad. Numbers 11:29 states, *"But Moses replied* [to Joshua and to perhaps the sixty-eight other elders], *'Are you jealous for my sake? I wish that all the Lord's people were prophets, and that the Lord would put his Spirit on them all!'"*

In the same spirit, Jesus answered His disciple's complaint saying, *"Don't stop them. No one who performs miracles in my name will soon speak evil of me. Anyone who is not against us is for us. If anyone gives you even a cup of water because you belong to the Messiah, I assure you, that person will be rewarded"* (Mark 9:39-41). Brothers and sisters, we are all on the same team! God help us from having a spirit of jealousy when He uses someone else in our field of ministry. Lord, keep us from wanting to quench another's vision or ministry.

A well-known pastor was told that another church had started in his town and was drawing more people than his own church. He saw the spirit of jealousy rising in the congregation, so he announced they were closing one of their Sunday night services and he then asked his congregation to join him at the other church to worship!

The late Bishop Raul Gonzales (a Teen Challenge Brooklyn graduate), founder of Youth Challenge Connecticut and Glory Chapel International in Hartford, had an unusual thing happen in the middle of raising funds for a new church building. A group of his church members decided to leave and began worshipping at another church in town. About a year later, the pastor of the other church came to see Bishop Gonzales. He handed him a rather large check and said, "This amount represents the tithe that the people who left your church have paid to my church over the past year. The Lord put it on my heart to bless you with this offering so you can put it towards your new building."

Who do you need to write a check to?

Who do we wrongly perceive is against us, when they are actually one of us?

A controversy arose during John the Baptist's ministry among some of his followers because more people were being baptized and following Jesus than John. John would not allow a division to arise between the two camps. He put the issue to rest by saying, *"He must increase, but I must decrease"* (John 3:30).

Luis Palau writes, *"One small seed of jealousy, once it takes root in the soil of the soul, can sprout overnight into a sprawling vine of poison ivy."*[1]

Joyce Meyers, in one of her sermons, said, *"You have to learn to be happy when other people get what you're still waiting for."*

The Apostle Paul gives us the right instruction in dealing with ministerial jealousy: *"Some are preaching out of jealousy and rivalry. But others preach about Christ with pure motives...but whether or not their motives are pure, the fact remains that the message about Christ is being preached, so I rejoice. And I will continue to rejoice"* (Philippians 1:15, 18).

"Whenever you attempt a good work, you will find another man doing the same kind of work, and probably doing it better. Envy them not" (Henry Drummond).[2]

My brother, David Wilkerson, writing in a sermon newsletter stated, *"We all have seeds of jealousy and envy in us. The question is, who among us will acknowledge it."*[3]

> *Love must be sincere. Hate what is evil; cling to what is good. Be devoted to one another in brotherly love. Honor one another above yourselves* (Romans 12:9-10).

A mature person is not threatened by other people's ministries or success.

5

ARE YOU LEAVING OR GOING?

Woe to the shepherd that leaveth the flock
(Zechariah 11:17, KJV).

The Lord will watch over your coming and going both
now and forevermore (Psalm 121:8, NIV).

Over the years, I have had staff members come to me to resign. Fortunately, most of the time, we have mutually agreed that it was God's leading for that worker to move on. However, on one such occasion, when I knew the person resigning was doing so out of the will of God, I asked, "Are you leaving or going?"

The response was, "Is there a difference?"

"Oh, there's a big difference," I replied. "If you're leaving because you're upset with me or the ministry, then you're leaving. But if God is calling you to go to another assignment, then it will be evident to all concerned, and you will be going with the blessings of everyone who has worked with you." I'm sad to say that person was leaving instead of going.

Leaving a church or ministry can often be very uncomfortable for everyone concerned. It does not need to be. Frankly, I have not always handled it well when people left under my leadership. At times, I have taken it too personal.

I think I am very sensitive to this matter of leaving rather than going, for I have found it hard on several occasions to know the difference for myself. My own failures in this area have made me aware of the importance of how we exit from a church or ministry. I do know *going* is much better than *leaving* when we have clearly heard God's voice calling us to go.

Abraham and Lot had to separate because their households became too large for them to stay together; their parting was amicable. Early on in my ministry I did not see that some of those who were under my leadership needed to move on because they were ready to be shepherds and leaders themselves. Remaining under my leadership would have held them back from fully expressing their gifts and talents. But I thought they just didn't want to minister under my guidance anymore.

There was a good transition of ministry when Moses handed the baton (perhaps I should say rod!) off to Joshua. Certainly Moses was not *leaving* but *going* on to his heavenly reward when the Lord said it was his time to go. *"Now Joshua son of Nun was filled with the spirit of wisdom because Moses had laid his hands on him. So the Israelites listened to him and did what the LORD had commanded Moses"* (Deuteronomy 34:9, NIV). The people listened to Joshua because of Moses' strong endorsement.

Leaving and Going at the Same Time?

In the book of Second Samuel, chapter seventeen, King David shows us how to handle both leaving and going at the same time. When his son Absalom took over the kingdom through a political and military coup, David left for his own safety and that of his household. This kind of leaving takes place all too frequently.

Often churches and para-church organizations have their leadership overthrown just like Absalom tried to do, and many soldiers of the cross have been deeply wounded as a result. David fled rather than lead the fight to defend himself; others fought in his stead and he was given back the kingdom. What wisdom it takes when an "Absalom" rises up in the church to take over, when it is not God's time for the leadership in place to leave. The point is that sometimes a group of workers, staff or members of a congregation believe it is time for a pastor or leader to leave when it is not God's will.

Other times, it may be necessary to *leave* and to *go* at the same time. By that I mean, if a church or ministry is going in the wrong direction or teaching false doctrine and someone tries to correct the situation, but cannot, then it's time to leave and go somewhere else to serve. Even Jesus taught His disciples when sending them out on a missions trip that they might not be welcomed with their message. Matthew 10:14 says, *"If any household or town refuses to welcome you or listen to you, shake off the dust of that place from your feet as you leave."*

There is a God-ordained *leaving* as the disciples were instructed to do. However, there is also a *leaving* which amounts to the forsaking of the call of God. Jacob left Isaac and Rebekah because of his and his mother's disobedience. Moses left Egypt for the wilderness because he tried to free his people by taking matters into his own hands—with a deadly instrument. The Prodigal son left his father's house to do his own thing, and ended up with nothing. This kind of *leaving* never ends on a good note.

The most famous account of *leaving*—moving in the wrong direction—was Jonah. He paid the fare to leave the path God chose for him because he would not pay the price of obedience to his calling. Job 6:18 says, *"Caravans turn aside from their routes; they go up into the wasteland and perish."* I have seen too many join modern-day caravans and *leave* the place of their assignment, instead of waiting for the Holy Spirit's call to *go*. Psalm 40 states: *"I waited patiently for the Lord, and He established my goings"* (vs. 1-2b, KJV).

Going in God's time and God's way brings blessings. *"For He guards the course of the just and protects the way of His faithful ones"* (Proverbs 2:8).

The most difficult challenge is when God calls you to go from a place without telling you where you are going. Such is the life of faith. Abraham was called to leave his home and go to a land that God would afterwards show him (See Hebrews 11:8). But the time and distance between *leaving* and knowing exactly where he was *going* was unknown when he first obeyed the Lord. For some of us, this is an exciting venture into the unknown. But for others, it tends to produce paralyzing fears. Many never arrive at the center of God's will for their lives because of fear and unbelief. God doesn't want it to be so.

6

SIGNS AND WONDERS

*You performed miraculous signs and
wonders in Egypt and have continued
them to this day, both in Israel and among
all mankind, and have gained the renown
that is still Yours* (Jeremiah 32:20).

*Jesus did many other miraculous signs in
the presence of his disciples which are not
recorded in this book* (John 20:30).

*Others, tempting Him,
sought a sign from heaven* (Luke 11:16).

I am sometimes asked by young Christians why
we do not see more signs and wonders in the church.
I ask the same questions. I do believe that in the
church as a whole there are still many signs, wonders
and miracles, even though they may not be evident in
many local churches. Sometimes we have to be
careful of what kind of sign we are looking for, and why.

When I was one of the pastors at Times Square
Church, I was asked this question from a new
convert. "Pastor, if we could go into a funeral home
and raise someone from the dead, people would flock
to the church." I explained that Lazarus was raised
from the dead and Jesus was raised from the dead
and there were very few new converts added to the
church. It was not until the Holy Spirit came and
revealed the truth of Jesus as the Messiah that the
church grew. Henry Drummond, when asked, *"Why
do you believe in miracles?"* answered, *"I see them*

every day in the changed lives of men and women who are saved and lifted through faith in the power of the living Christ."[1]

Sign and wonders do validate the message of the Gospel. *"And God verified the message by signs and wonders and by various miracles and by giving gifts of the Holy Spirit whenever He chose to do so"* (Hebrews 2:4). Centuries ago, St. Augustine wrote, *"I should not be a Christian but for miracles."*[2] I once heard Katherine Kuhlman say, *"Everything that happened in the early church, we have a right to expect today."*[3] It is perfectly clear that in New Testament times the Gospel was authenticated by signs, wonders and miracles of various characters and descriptions. Was it only meant to be true for the early church? The Scriptures never anywhere say these things were temporary—never! There is no such statement anywhere.

Oh, that there were more miracles today of healing, of demons cast out, and other New Testament wonders and miracles. At times, I am put to shame by Christians, especially in third world countries, who believe God for both simple and big miracles in their lives. Once, I asked a Christian brother from England who was in ministry in Mexico why there were so many miracles of healing in the church there. His answer was simple: "There is little adequate health care here, and when it's available, most of these people cannot afford it. So they trust God."

There is another aspect of "signs and wonders" that needs to be addressed. If we have to keep asking God for signs to bolster our faith, it can be an indication of a lack of trust in Him. The teachers of the law and the Pharisees kept asking Jesus to show them miracles as a sign that He came from God, even after Jesus had already shown them many such signs. His reply was that *"...only an evil, faithless generation would ask for a miraculous sign"* (Matthew 12:38-39).

It seems to be a principle in Scripture that signs and wonders follow them that believe, but once we are rooted in our faith, we should not need to follow after signs and wonders. Yet many do! Healing meetings are full of people who seek after a sign, and often the evangelist obliges them by claiming healings and miracles that are in the eyes of the beholder, but not actually proven.

> *There are too many people who expect God to work by miracle what God expects people to work by muscle* (W. Galloway Tyson).[4] *The spectacular and the supernatural are not necessarily related to each other* (Steve Sampson).[5]

Signs Still Follow Those Who Believe

What then does the Scripture mean when it says in Mark 16:17, *"These signs shall follow those who believe?"* I believe it means just what it says. When signs are sought because of a need for divine intervention to meet a physical, financial or other type of need, rather than seeking a sign of proof for our faith, then the motive is right.

Signs and wonders are for unbelievers as much as for believers. In Acts 2:22, Peter said that signs and wonders are heaven's endorsement of Jesus. They also were endorsements of the apostles (Acts 2:43); they gave the early disciples boldness in the face of persecution (Acts 4:27-31); they drew many to Christ and helped build the church (Acts 5:12-16).

Signs and wonders surely helped to spread the Gospel (Acts 8:4-17). When a sign or wonder is manufactured, or if they are sought as one might want to see a magic act, this fulfills Jesus' warning that an *"evil generation"* seeks after signs. *"It is almost impossible to exaggerate the proneness of the human mind to take miracles as evidence and to seek for miracles as evidence"* (Matthew Arnold.)[6]

Tim Keller writes in his book, *The Reason for God*, that *"...if there is a Creator God, there is nothing illogical at all about the possibility of miracles. After all, if He created everything out of nothing, it would hardly be a problem for Him to rearrange parts of it when He wishes."*[7] I am not one of those who believe that miracles ceased after the days of the apostles in the book of Acts. However, I am also not one who, like a spiritual child, needs constant reassurances and proof of God's love and care by asking for and looking for "signs" that are not true "signs."

Charles Spurgeon once said that the Lord's miracles were intended as parables, that is, to instruct, as well as to impress. *"They are sermons to the eye, just as his spoken discourses were sermons for the ear."*[8]

7

PARA-CHRISTIANS

*I appointed you to go and produce fruit that
will last* (John 15:16).

*Strengthening the disciples and
encouraging them to remain true to the faith*
(Acts 14:22).

I was privileged to begin my ministry at a time when a number of specialized ministries were birthed. I'll mention just a few of them: The Navigators, Intervarsity Press, Youth With A Mission, Prison Fellowship, Focus on the Family, Trinity Broadcasting Network and of course, Teen Challenge. These organizations came alongside the church and became known as para-church ministries (para meaning outside or alongside).

Each of these mentioned, (and numerous others) have a specifically defined purpose for ministry, often doing what a local church is unable to do. Countless souls have found Christ through these ministries. They reach a variety of people groups because of their singular focus, such as college and university students, families, prisoners, people with life-controlling problems, unreached people in many lands, and the poor.

In my work with drug addicts, I have discovered that the very strength of our ministry—our focus on evangelizing and discipling addicts—was also our weakness if we did not connect converts to the local church.

Any and all evangelism efforts ought to have as a part of the strategy the incorporating of converts into a local church. Many evangelistic organizations, such as the Billy Graham Evangelistic Association, work diligently to make sure local churches are an integral part of the planning and follow up of their evangelistic outreaches. Without the partnership between the para-church and the local church, the result is what I call "para-Christians"—people who become spiritual vagabonds, forever looking for a spiritual home.

Testimonies abound of someone finding Christ through a television ministry or any of the organizations mentioned above, and then joining a local church. This should be the end result of all para-church ministries. Sadly, it does not happen in enough cases.

Hit-And-Run Evangelism

There is too much of what I call "hit-and-run evangelism." Whenever an evangelistic campaign is done as a stand-alone effort without local church involvement, there may be decisions for Christ, but few disciples of Christ. Of course, on a personal level, it is always right to share Christ one-on-one with someone in the course of daily activities in which there may be no opportunity for follow-up. In such cases, one has to trust the power of the Word and the Holy Spirit to lead that person to a church.

However, when an outreach is conducted on a larger scale, and there is no bridge provided for a possible new convert to be connected to a local church, the outreach cannot be deemed successful in my estimation.

Of course, it should also be pointed out that in some places/countries there may not be local churches for converts to attend. This requires evangelism efforts for the purpose of church planting. Also, there are times when responding to a national crisis means focusing primarily upon meeting the need for food, shelter and medical care. In this case, humanitarian needs should be done in the name of Christ, even when evangelizing is not immediately possible. Fortunately, seeds are sown that can produce results at a later time and place.

The normative pattern in the New Testament was *"The Lord added to the church such as should be saved"* (Acts 2:47, KJV). As the vine is to the branches, so the church and the para-church should represent Christ to the new convert.

In past decades, large para-church ministries have often overshadowed the local church. However, there seems to be a return to the rightful place of the church in relationship to specialized ministries. I have spent most of my ministry as a para-church leader trying to forge the vital partnership between outreach and intake, which is another way of saying para-church and church.

All evangelism should have, as its ultimate purpose, the bringing of lost souls into the fellowship of the church. And by the "church" I do not just mean the church universal, but a specific local church. In my early days, conducting outreach evangelism, sending out witnessing teams on the streets and having open air meetings, I blamed the church for not following up with the converts. The truth was we did not include churches in our planning, usually involving the church only as an afterthought. Then we expected them to know when to step in to follow-up on our efforts.

For years, I proclaimed that Teen Challenge was an "arm of the church" only to realize that we were more like an arm *detached from a body.* We began correcting that by teaching young converts the importance and purpose of the local church and trying to have our converts/students attend one specific church as much as possible.

Some para-church organizations make no effort to connect their converts to the church and end up creating spiritual vagabonds floating about, looking for a spiritual home. It's been my privilege to try to correct this and teach some para-church leaders to plant churches when it is possible.

Previously, I shared in my book, *Within a Yard of Hell:*

> *Too often the approach of organized evangelistic endeavors to follow up is that of "adoption" rather than "parenting." In adoption, the person led to the Lord is referred to someone else who may not know (or care) about nurturing "babes" in Christ. This "name referral" system is not unlike placing a newborn on some random doorstep, ringing the doorbell, then running off, hoping the child will be cared for. Fewer people respond to the task of "fathering"—the term Paul used for aftercare discipleship. Evangelism seems so much more rewarding, exciting, and glamorous than discipling—perhaps it's the difference between the excitement over the birth of a newborn baby in contrast to caring for the same child in its "terrible twos."*[1]

It may be an overstatement to compare discipling someone from spiritual infancy to spiritual maturity to the rearing of a strong-willed child, but most would agree that the task of evangelism is not finished unless it's connected to helping the convert to grow up spiritually (See Ephesians 2:21-22; 4:15). And that includes being incorporated into a local church.

> *Sometimes, friends, there comes a harvest. Someday there is a payoff. Someday sinners become saints. And between now and then, we get to keep spreading the message. We get to keep playing the message. We get to keep playing the roles we are meant to play. We get to keep planting seeds, trusting God will give the increase. Because in due time, oh, the increase He brings* (Bill Hybels).[2]

PART TWO
Advice to My Fellow Leaders

8
AUTHORITY

Jesus called them [His disciples] *together and said, "You know that those who are regarded as rulers of the Gentiles lord it over them, and their high officials exercise authority over them. Not so with you"* (Mark 10:42-43a).

I was clueless for years about how to use the personal authority given to me in ministry positions of overseeing staff, working with boards and lay people. Whether I used my authority properly or improperly, I was unaware of the effect I was having on others. Bible College never taught me about the use of personal or pastoral authority and the difference between the two. I learned it the hard way, and slowly. All authority comes from God, but He entrusts ministry authority into human hands.

After years of service, I am now aware of the influence I can wield as one who is in a position of authority in ministry. Hopefully, I now use it correctly more often than not.

I have learned that if I have to tell someone I am *the boss* or *in charge,* then I'm operating from a position of insecurity. It's like the pastor who put in his sermon notes this highlight beside a certain point: "Shout really loud!—Weak point!" Some leaders shout too loud, trying to prove they are the leader—perhaps trying to convince themselves as well. Weak leaders do things that reveal their insecurity—they pick other weak leaders to serve with them, and consistently remind others that they are in charge.

There are many tests by which a gentleman may be known; but there is one that never fails—how does he exercise power over those subordinate to him? (Samuel Smiles).[1]

Authority is Always Tested

Jesus is our biblical model. He spoke and led with firm authority. *"He taught as one who had authority, and not as their teachers"* (Matthew 7:29). They had never seen such authority tempered with grace and gentleness before. Jesus' first great test was when Satan tempted Him into misusing His power and authority (See Matthew 4:1-11). An abuse of authority is often decried in the Scriptures. Jeremiah 5:31 says, *"The prophets prophesy lies, the priests rule by their own authority, and my people love it this way. But what will you do in the end?"*

A staff member came to me once and complained that the students under his charge would not listen to him. "Brother Don, tell them that they have to respect my authority!"

"I cannot do that," I replied. "You have to earn it."

Jesus also said, *"You've observed how godless rulers throw their weight around, how quickly a little power goes to their heads. It's not going to be that way with you. Whoever wants to be great must become a servant. Whoever wants to be first among you must be your slave"* (Matthew 20:25-27, The Message). There are so many old proverbs that address the issue of authority, such as, *"If you wish to know what a man is, place him in authority"* (Author unknown). And another; "Authority without wisdom is like a heavy *axe without an edge, fitter to bruise than polish"* (Anne Bradstreet).[2]

Paul, the Apostle, gives us two good points about authority in relationship to those we serve. First, he exhorts us to use it to build people up: *"For even if I boast somewhat freely about the authority the Lord gave us for building you up rather than tearing you down, I will not be ashamed of it"* (2 Corinthians 10:8). Second, he reminds us not to be harsh when using it. *"This is why I write these things when I am absent, that when I come I may not have to be harsh in my use of authority—the authority the Lord gave me for building you up, not for tearing you down"* (2 Corinthians 13:10). Plato said, *"The wisest have the most authority."* It is a wise and mature leader who knows when, where, how and with whom to exercise authority.

I would like to add one more word: Stay humble when others recognize and respect your authority. *Authority* must be wedded to *humility*, or it becomes arrogance and pride.

Authority in My Youth

I began preaching at the age of sixteen. Sometimes I struggled when people seemed to disrespect me because of my youth. My father told me often, *"Son, let no man despise your youth."* I always understood the authority of the Word spoken under the anointing of the Holy Spirit. However, it took me some years to know how to use ministerial authority with firmness and grace.

Young leaders need to follow Paul's instructions to Timothy: *"Don't let anyone look down on you because you are young, but set an example for the believers in speech, in conduct, in love, in faith and in purity"* (1Timothy 4:12). Paul encouraged young Titus, whom he left on the island of Crete to help set the house churches in order. It was not an easy task, as the Cretes had an unsavory reputation (See Titus 1:12-14). Paul instructed Titus how to rightly use godly authority: *"You must teach these things and encourage people to do them, correcting them when necessary. You have the authority to do this, so don't let anyone ignore you or disregard you"* (Titus 2:15). At any age, this is good advice!

Using Conferred (or Delegated) Authority

Many leaders do not know how to use conferred authority. When under-shepherds and those who serve directly under an overseer carry out directives, they are exercising *conferred authority.* This too needs to be done in a way that truly reflects the will *and character* of the leader. Too often, I have seen a leader hurt by the misuse of authority by those serving under him or her. They may have communicated what the leader wanted done, but in a different manner or heart attitude than the person they served. Tone of voice and body language is communication. The leader with a heart of love will communicate authority with that same love.

Jesus conferred authority to His disciples, and He expected them to use it as humble servants and not like the Gentile leaders who lorded over others (See Luke 22:25-30). All who serve such a vital part as pastors and leaders would do well to read these passages carefully from the Gospel of Luke.

I am also aware that when I do give someone authority, I need to make it public. The Lord told Moses to give some of his authority to Joshua, and to do it publicly (See Numbers 27:18-23). Leaders need to know when to totally pass on their authority, (as Moses did with Joshua) or to simply delegate some aspects of authority to assistants. If it is not done openly, as Moses was instructed by God to do, then it makes it difficult for the one given the authority to exercise it.

All who wield authority in church and ministry must always know that the source of all authority comes from God; not the pulpit, not the denominational headquarters or department heads; not the pastor or executive director, president, CEO or whatever the title. *"He called his twelve disciples and gave them authority"* (Matthew 10:1). Paul stated in Colossians that all authority for church leadership comes from Christ: *"For in Christ all the fullness of the Deity lives in bodily form, and you have been given fullness in Christ, who is the head over every power and authority"* (2:9-10).

> *No man is worthy to rule until he has been ruled; no man can lead until he has given himself to leadership greater than his own* (Catherine Marshall).[3]

9

SPIRITUAL GIFT MIX

The body of Christ...has many different parts,
not just one part (1 Corinthians 12:12, 14).

As a young man growing up in the church, I remember we had "Revival Meetings" with guest speakers who would minister through the week. As the pastor, my father learned from his congregation the importance of having different spiritual gifts evident in these visiting preachers.

After one series of meetings, the elders and deacons came to my father and said, "Pastor, we would rather have heard you preach this week." My dad appreciated the compliment, but he immediately realized he'd invited a speaker with a pastoral gift very similar to his own. "I need someone to minister in the church who brings a different gifting than what God has given me," my father wisely noted. From then on, speakers were invited with spiritual gifts that differed from his to benefit the congregation: evangelists, teachers, and those with prophetic or healing gifts.

From this experience, I learned the importance of having a good gift mix of those on the ministry team and staff. After all, the diversity of spiritual gifts represents Jesus more fully. He embodied all those gifts in His life and ministry. And certainly none of the gifts should be elevated above the others. Romans 12:6 reminds us, *"We have different gifts according to the grace given us."*

In the discipleship of students at Teen Challenge, I need a staff team with a good gift mix. If every staff member had the gift of mercy, the students would take advantage of them and not be given proper discipline. If every staff member had the gift of discernment, the discipline might be too critical or harsh. If every staff member had the gift of leadership, there would be a conflict of ideas, or "too many cooks that would spoil the broth!"

Biblical Examples

In the book of Acts, Paul and Barnabas are excellent examples of different gifts, both working well together and then moving into conflict. Barnabas was the encourager, probably with the gift of mercy. Paul was a teacher (among his other gifts) and he exercised great discernment. They worked for some time spreading the Gospel of Christ until they disagreed over John Mark's role in their ministry. Barnabas' gift of mercy was at odds with Paul's discernment! The conflict was directly related to their God-given gifts of the Spirit for ministry (See Acts 15:36-40).

In the Old Testament, when a remnant of the Jews returned to Jerusalem from Babylonian captivity, God called two men with both similar and different spiritual gifts to rebuild God's people, spiritually and physically. Ezra was called first in the rebuilding of the Temple. He was a man of faith who was also unwilling to compromise the truths taught in God's Word as he led the Hebrew people to rebuild the house of God. *"For Ezra had devoted himself to the study and observance of the Law of the Lord, and to teaching its decrees and laws in Israel"* (Ezra 7:10).

Later, Nehemiah was called from Babylon to return to Jerusalem to rebuild the city's walls. He had the gifts of administration, organization, leadership and discernment; things needed in the rebuilding of the wall of Jerusalem in the midst of great opposition. When some politicians tried to stop the project, Nehemiah had the determination and wisdom to stay on the wall and not come down to the level of his enemies. He cried out in response to their threats and harassment, *"Why should the work stop while I leave it and come down to you?"* (Nehemiah 6:3)

We Are Many Parts

The human body has many parts, but the many parts make up one body. So it is with the body of Christ...Yes, the body has many different parts, not just one part (1 Corinthians 12:12, 14. See also 1 Corinthians 12:27-31).

A football team cannot have more than one main quarterback. A basketball team that has five point guards would need to play with five basketballs! And a church or ministry team needs the right mixture of spiritual gifts. *"A spiritual gift is given to each of us so we can help each other"* (1 Corinthians 12:7). In interviewing prospective staff, I always try to find out what the person's gift is. Many people in ministry have not yet discovered it! But a series of questions usually helps me uncover their spiritual gifts.

I have always referred to staff and workers under my leadership as being a team. It is not a biblical word, but it is a biblical principle. I am convinced that many staff issues and differences resulting in resignations and ill feelings are due to having too many people with the same gifts on board. It is time we learned the importance of all the spiritual gifts, recognizing that a church shouldn't have a body with too many feet or too many hands and not enough of the other essential body parts.

"Suppose the whole body were an eye—how would you hear?" (1 Corinthians 12:17). If the eye represents the gift of discernment and the ear represents the gift of mercy (to show mercy, one must be a good listener), for the church to have eyes without ears would be a hindrance to the spiritual growth of the whole body.

The purpose of the five-fold gifts listed in Ephesians 4:11 is so that, *"we* [the church] *all come to such unity in our faith and knowledge of God's Son that we will be mature in the Lord, measuring up to the full and complete standard of Christ* (Ephesians 4:13).

J. E. O' Day, in a small booklet I recommend entitled, *Discovering Your Spiritual Gifts,* writes:

> *Christians sometimes fall short in actually using their gifts. Many are standing on first base when instead, they need to be running the bases. One reason is they are unaware of their spiritual gifts.*[1]

O' Day suggests that a church or ministry might do well to take an inventory of its full-time and volunteer workers in respect to their spiritual gift or gifts. (We usually have more than one gift.)

Of course, there are times when workers need to serve in an area that doesn't match their gifting. I always encourage them to serve there as "unto the Lord" until the person with the right gift comes along to take their place. However, the greatest joy and success in service for the Lord is when our gifts match our tasks.

When Timothy may have been discouraged by the challenges he faced while leading the church at Ephesus, (backslidings, false teachings, etc.) Paul instructed him to remember the pastoral gifts that accompanied his calling: *"Wherefore I put thee in remembrance that thou stir up the gift of God, which is in thee by the putting on of my hands"* (2 Timothy 1:6, KJV). Timothy had the gift of a pastor/teacher.

Every believer has at least one spiritual gift. They need to know, or be taught, what it is and encouraged to use it. Leaders need to be like coaches and managers, guiding believers to use their gifts in the church for the edification of the whole Body.

> *The gifts are not in any way confined to the elders or to any other group separated from the rest of the congregation. It is high time that the church today got back to the New Testament and asked serious questions about their understanding of ordination to the ministry, which in practice tends to confine most forms of ministry to a limited group of ordained people. God doesn't appear to be bound by such limits in bestowing His gifts* (I. Howard Marshall).[2]

> *What was special about the new dispensation was that, first of all, these gifts were not confined to any one group of people but extended to all—male and female, young and old. Secondly, these supernatural endowments were wonderfully diverse* (Charles Hodge).[3]

10
THE UNTITLED LEADER

The greatest among you must be a servant.
But those who exalt themselves will be humbled,
and those who humble themselves will be exalted
(Matthew 23:11-12).

I do not find in the Bible that Abraham, Isaac or Jacob called attention to themselves through a title, although they were Patriarchs. Moses certainly deserved some title, yet none was assigned to him; nor Aaron or Joshua; nor are titles given for the numerous workers who set up and took down the Tabernacle during the wilderness journey of the children of Israel.

> *These...were responsible for the care of the frames supporting the Tabernacle, the crossbars, the pillars, the bases, and all the equipment related to their use* (Numbers 3:36).

Later the titles of Judge, King, Prophet and Priest were given to men and women in leadership roles in the Old Testament. However, most people mentioned in the Bible had no title, even if they held important positions.

I have never liked titles for myself, although I realize they are necessary. I have held titles such as Reverend, Pastor, Director, Executive Director and President. However, I always knew that my title did not define me. My favorite titles, if I had to choose, are Christian, husband, father, and now in my later years, Pop Pop (grandfather).

A title can be important, especially when whoever holds it fulfills the function and role behind that title. Paul the Apostle vigorously defended his office as an apostle. However, most often he simply called himself a "servant/slave of Jesus Christ." Not everyone has a title or needs one. Some of my best workers never held an official title.

The only time the word addicted is used in the Bible is in 1 Corinthians 16:15 when Paul talks about the house of Stephanas that, *"They have addicted themselves to the ministry of the saints"* (KJV). Paul mentions no titles in association with their names, though they may have had them. He went on to say that the believers in this house church should be given *"proper honor"* because they served so well (See 1 Corinthians 15:18).

Mark Sanborn, in his book, *You Don't Need a Title to Be a Leader,* tells of an organization that needed someone to head up an important project. The female candidate selected was told they could not make her the director of the project. She responded by saying, *"That's alright. I don't need a title to be a leader."*[1]

Right now, as I write this, there is a big controversy in the New York City public school system as to how to get rid of ineffective teachers. Apparently, the title "teacher" does not automatically make one a true teacher from whom students can actually learn. Some of my best teachers never actually held that title.

In Romans 16, Paul mentions some untitled people who helped him in the work of God. He refers to them as saints, helpers, kinsmen, chosen, fellow workers, hosts, and brothers. Perhaps some of these did have official titles, but Paul identified them by *relationship* instead of by *position* or title.

Positive Influence Produces Results

John Maxwell defines a leader as someone with *positive influence*.[2] Some of the leaders I have worked with have been people of influence as intercessors, prayer warriors, financial givers, servants with the gift of helps, encouragers, peacemakers, and connectors. The latter are those who know how to bring people together. These are the behind-the-scenes, backstage people who make it possible for those who are upfront leaders to fulfill God's calling in ministry. These are people who define what humility is: It isn't thinking less of yourself. It is thinking of yourself *less.*

In some cultures, titles are very important. If the titleholder fulfills the job description associated with the title, this is good; but some merely want to have a title for the prestige that goes with it. It can be a mistake to give some people a title, for they take it far too seriously and become entrenched in their position. They try to wield control over others just because of that title. I have seen foot soldiers vie for a position that carries a coveted title, and then they turn around and undermine their leaders.

Many pastors have lived with the stress of a deacon who thought his or her title and position entitled them to control the pastor and the church. Similarly, I have seen para-church organizations with board members who felt that their role was to keep their leader in check, rather than help facilitate his vision. Pastors and leaders need accountability, but they do not need undue scrutiny.

It's the untitled people who bless churches and organizations by their selfless service. Most of them could care less about a title. They just want to get the job done, and do it well. John Maxwell says of leadership, "It's not about position, but production."[3]

Some of the great people of influence who have made huge differences in society and had humanitarian or evangelistic impact, are not known by their title, though they had one. The name Billy Graham will always be associated with soul winning and evangelism. Mother Theresa was a nun of a Catholic Sisterhood order, but the term Mother defines her as someone who cared for the poor and suffering. Martin Luther King, Jr. led a movement against prejudice and racism. He was a reverend and doctor, but no title is necessary to characterize his influence.

It is impossible for a title or an organizational chart to reflect all of the many people who function as leaders or exert leadership throughout the organization. That is why I call such people non-titled leaders. They may or may not have direct responsibility to lead others, yet every day they positively influence and lead those around them.

Consider some unknown persons in the Bible whom God used: (1) the servant girl who influenced Naaman, commander of King Aram's army, to go to Elisha to seek healing for his leprosy (See Second Kings 5). (2) The lad with a lunch that fed 5,000 (See John 6). He was the right person, in the right place, at the right time. I have had hundreds of such people help further the work of God, just like that lad. (3) A Samaritan woman simply known as "the woman at the well" who brought a whole village to Christ (See John 4). (4) The innkeeper who gave Mary and Joseph a stable for the Christ child to be born (See Luke 2). (5) The innkeeper that took in the man brought to him by the Good Samaritan; and there are many more!

Each of them had either influence or something to give to be used for the work of God.

Characteristics of Untitled Leaders

Paul wrote some very strong admonitions to the church at Corinth. The church still had those who acted with a servant's heart, and he commended them for how they refreshed Titus' spirit (See 2 Corinthians 7:13-16). These are the kind of untitled people and leaders all churches and ministries need. Whether the believers Paul talks about were titled as leaders we don't know, but no church or ministry can succeed without them.

I once heard the late John Wimber, founder of the Vineyard Churches, say that an elder is someone who "elds." He explained, "Look around the church and see those who people go to for prayer, counsel and advice." He called that "eld-ing," a term similar to that of an elder. Yet, they were not necessarily a titled elder, but usually an untitled one.

Here are some characteristics of untitled leaders:
1. They see the small stuff that needs to be done.
2. They are great encouragers.
3. They do what they do regardless of appreciation shown to them.
4. They don't wait to be told to do something—they just do it.
5. They like to come alongside the titled leaders to help him, or her, to fulfill their calling.
6. Some work best alone, but others are good at motivating people to get involved.
7. They tactfully show titled leaders where they might have a blind spot.

8. They are generally very loyal.
9. Other people are drawn to them.
10. They're problem solvers, not problem complainers.

The bottom line is that influence and inspiration come from *the person,* not *the position.*

Jill Briscoe, wrote: "You may not be involved in full-time ministry; and yet, if you are a believer, your basic job description is the same as mine. It is to be full of the Holy Spirit and to pour yourself out to others in love and ministry, trusting in the Spirit to make it possible."[4]

In the kingdom of God, there is no role unimportant and no job trivial. It is good for the one doing a seemingly trivial task to recognize this, as well as those assigning the task.

> *Do you see a man skilled in his work? He will serve before kings; he will not serve before obscure men* (Proverbs 22:29, NIV).

It's amazing what someone can do, small or great, if they don't care who gets the credit. However, in God's sight, all service is rewarded. The doing of it, in and of itself, is a reward. Heaven does take note of all service done for Christ by titled leaders and by untitled ones!

11

EVERYONE NEEDS AN "AND"

This letter is from Paul and Timothy,
slaves of Jesus Christ (Philippians 1:1).

Sometimes simple words can leap off the pages of the Bible and speak volumes to us. It happened to me while reading Paul's epistles. He uses the word "and" as a conjunction between two nouns seven different times at the beginning of his letters.

Most of Paul's "ands" were connected to Timothy. In 2 Corinthians, Philippians, Colossians, 1 and 2 Thessalonians, and Philemon Paul says the letter is from him *and* Timothy. In two epistles (1 and 2 Thessalonians), he adds *and Silas,* and in 1 Corinthians it says, *"From Paul...and from our brother Sostenes."*

Consider some other important co-workers in scripture: Moses *and* Aaron, Moses *and* Miriam, Moses *and* Joshua, Caleb *and* Joshua, Abraham *and* Sarah, David *and* Jonathan, Elijah *and* Elisha, Jesus *and* His disciples, Paul *and* Barnabas. God works through individuals *and* partnerships! Solomon wrote, *"Two people are better off than one, for they can help each other succeed. If one person falls, the other can reach out and help. But someone who falls alone is in real trouble"* (Ecclesiastes 4:10).

Who is Your "And"?

We all need an *and* in life and in ministry. My main "and" is my wife. Don *and* Cindy are a team.

I was privileged for years to be linked to my late brother, David in the founding of Teen Challenge and Times Square Church. When I'm mentioned in the same sentence with my brother, "David *and* Don" it is such a great honor, not just because we are biological brothers, but also partners in the founding of two outstanding ministries.

I could make a long list of many other "ands" in my life. Ministry is not for lone rangers; it must be a shared experience. Insecure leaders often fear partnerships, as they do not want to share either the burden or the credit for what is accomplished.

Sometimes we can be at the front end of the "and". Sometimes at the back end. Let me explain. In the book of Acts, up to the 13th chapter, whenever Barnabas and Paul are mentioned, Barnabas' name is always listed first. But after the church leaders at Antioch laid hands on them and they were sent out by the Holy Spirit, whenever Barnabas is mentioned, Paul's name comes first (Acts 13:4).

When the teacher becomes the student of the one he once taught, it means the teacher has done a very good job. My father was asked how it felt to have two sons who could out-preach him. It was meant as a compliment to my father, and he received it that way. His response was to say, "What kind of a father would I be if I cannot raise sons that can out-do me?"

Sometimes those whom we disciple and teach in the church and in ministry do great exploits beyond what their pastor/teacher has done. I enjoy sitting and listening to some of my spiritual sons and daughters minister the Word of God. During those moments, I experience what my own father felt when he heard my brother David or me preach from the pulpit.

A. W. Tozer writes: "The true leader will have no desire to lord it over God's heritage, but will be humble, gentle, self-sacrificing and altogether as ready to follow as to lead when the Spirit makes it clear that a wiser and more gifted man than himself has appeared."[1] If King Saul could only have recognized the anointing on David, the history of Israel in the days of the kings might have turned out differently.

The list of partnerships in biblical times is noteworthy. Besides the ones we already mentioned there is: Jacob *and* Esau (their relationship ended well), Deborah *and* Barak, David *and* Joab, Mary *and* Martha, Peter, James *and* John. When a church or ministry sees leaders working together as a team and in unity, this becomes contagious. Pastors and leaders are to lead the way in this.

> *May the God who gives endurance and encouragement give you a spirit of unity among yourselves as you follow Christ Jesus* (Romans 15:5).

A. W. Tozer taught that when the church prays for the Holy Spirit to come so that we be "one," we actually have this backwards. "He does not come to make us a united people. The Holy Spirit comes BECAUSE we are a united people. Our prayer should be more like, 'Lord, help us to get united in order that the [Holy Spirit's] blessing might flow and there might be an outpouring of oil and dew and life.'"[2] Unity begins in our closest relationships in the body of Christ, and that can create a ripple effect to the entire body.

So, who is your "and"? This question is of utmost importance. Maybe he or she is right beside you, although you have not yet recognized them.

12

THE "OTHER" CURRICULUM

You are our epistle written in our hearts,
known and read by all men
(2 Corinthians 3:2, NKJV).

There are, or should be, within every local church and in every faith-based rehab program two curriculums, and both are equally important. The first is in the formal classroom where the written curriculum is taught, and the second is how we live our lives before our students and congregations. Because I write to both pastors and faith-based rehab programs, I include the following specifically for rehab programs: In these days when the students have to be used for outside work and fundraising, it's important that they not get cheated out of their classroom studies. Also, novices should not be used to teach these classes. What has separated Teen Challenge from other faith-based programs is our commitment to have relevant Bible classes for our students.

Local churches that do not provide discipleship classroom education will not produce strong disciples; and they will lose believers who are looking for more in-depth teaching than what comes from the pulpit. However, even the best Christian education programs can miss a vital part of discipleship if they do not recognize the importance of what I call the "other curriculum." If attention and commitment is not given to this, it can undue everything taught in the classroom. Recognizing this other curriculum is basic 101 Christianity. Paul says it all in this verse: "You are our epistle written in our hearts, known and read by all men. Clearly you are an epistle of Christ, ministered by us, written not with ink, but by the Spirit of the living God, not on tablets of stone but on tablets of the flesh, that is, of the heart" (2 Corinthians 3:2-3, NKJV).

It's an old expression, but still true that people need to see a sermon, and not just hear one. If all the church or rehab program staff workers are not living epistles, this creates confusion, distrust, and possible anger within the students. One of the problems in programs which use so many graduates as staff is that for some reason, as soon as they cross over from student to staff, they often go into neutral, spiritually. Worse is when they order students around and no longer want to get their hands dirty; that is, they cease to become servants and want to become lords.

What is taught in the classroom, preached from the pulpit, or shared in counseling sessions needs to be backed up and reinforced by staff, from the kitchen to the classroom and by each worker in between those two places. Maybe what should be done besides grading the students in their classwork is have the students grade the staff as living epistles! Graduates that become staff and do not carry around a towel of servanthood, as Jesus did with and for His disciples, do not understand what it takes to be a true leader.

Of course, we cannot expect perfection in ourselves, or anyone else. But there are biblical standards that all of us need to live up to on a daily basis; especially in an environment in which students and staff work so closely together. The potential for good examples is so powerful in such an environment, as well as the potential for bad ones.

You cannot put straight in others what is warped in yourself. Albert Schweitzer said, *"Example is not the main thing in influencing others. It is the only thing."*[1] In both church life and community life such as Teen Challenge, it is often the case that Christians reach a certain level of spiritual growth and become stagnant and spiritually stationary. However, developing the fruit of the Spirit is, or should be, a lifelong process.

Here is something to think about—for me as well as you! If God wrote a book about me or you, in what section would it be placed in a Barnes and Noble bookstore? Fiction or non-fiction? Humorous? Ancient history? Religion? Politics? Or Current Affairs, perhaps. I'd hope that mine would be in the latter, to denote that my relationship with God and my spiritual growth is on-going and up-to-date.

If you are a leader, here is something you can challenge your staff with: *"Not as though I had already attained, either were already perfect..."* (Philippians 3:12) Since Paul said he had not yet attained, where does that leave the rest of us? With a lot of catching up to do!

Paul continues in Philippians 3:12 saying, "I follow after..." (KJV) This is an interesting word when looked at in the original Greek. It is a fiercely aggressive word. In Greek literature it was used in respect to hunting, and to pursue, to chase and to kill. Wow!

Quoting from *Sparkling Gems* by Rick Renner,

It is the picture of an outdoorsman who is so determined to follow after and hunt down an animal and that he will stop at nothing to pursue, chase, track down, and ultimately get his game! Do hunters accidently bag their game, or do they strategize in their plans to get a good one each hunting season? Hunter's strategize![2]

I know this, not from personal experience, but because my wife, who is from Vermont, has five brothers, and come deer season, they are committed to the sport of deer hunting. They dream! They talk to other hunters about the best places to hunt! They dress in camouflaged clothing, then they perch themselves high up in tree branches and wait hours upon hours for an unlucky deer to walk into their area. Once the deer comes in range, they shoot to kill. They have followed after their prey.

This is exactly what Paul writes when he said he followed after, so he might *"apprehend that for which I have been apprehended of Christ Jesus."* Quoting again from *Sparkling Gems*:

> *The apostle Paul strategized, planned, studied, and ardently followed after the call of God on his life. You could say that he hunted, hounded and stalked the call of God with all his heart, never stopping until he could say 'I got my game!' For you to achieve what God has planned for your life, it will likewise require a fierce determination to keep pressing ahead. You can never stop until every part of your God-given assignment has been fulfilled. Jogging along in a comfortable pace will never get you where you need to go.*[3]

Joshua 3:3 says, *"When you see the ark* (an Old Testament symbol of Christ), *then you shall set out from that place, and go after it."*

> *You will never arrive if you don't set out.*
> *The tragedy of life is not that it ends soon,*
> *but that we wait too long for it to begin* (W.
> M. Lewis).[4]

Let's wholeheartedly pursue after Christ and follow Paul's example, knowing that our lives are part of the curriculum others are learning from—either affirming or denying the teachings of Scripture.

13

LOSING ONE'S VOICE

And now you will be silent and not able to speak until the day this happens, because you did not believe my words, which will come true at their proper time (Luke 1:20).

The fear of God came on me during a counseling session with a couple having marital problems. The husband had committed adultery and the two were trying to bring about reconciliation. As we spoke, I noted the husband said very little. He was humbled and expressed remorse; but beyond that, he had very little to say. That's when one of the saddest results of sin became real to me. This husband, father and church member had lost his voice. Only his actions over time could restore his reputation, the trust of his family, and his voice.

As I witnessed this man's loss of voice, I inwardly said to the Lord, *"I don't ever want to lose my voice."*

I know a mother who earnestly begged her son to stop using drugs and get some help. He'd make promise after promise to change, but never actually took any action to do something about his addiction. Each time, he begged for one more chance, saying, "Mom, I will change."

Finally, his mother declared, "You need to leave this house! I can't deal with this anymore! I don't want to hear another word out of you."

The son had lost his voice. Habitual sin silences one's voice.

When Leaders Lose Their Voice

In the earlier years of his life, when Moses tried to right the wrongs of Egypt towards his people and he killed an Egyptian in anger, he lost his voice before Pharaoh and his people. It was forty years before God gave him a voice back.

When Miriam, Moses' sister, challenged her brother's authority, she lost her voice; as did their brother, Aaron, for joining her in touching God's anointed (See Numbers 12:1-2). They lost their positions of authority and faced God's discipline. It took Moses' prayerful intervention before God for Miriam and Aaron to be restored to the congregation (Numbers 12:13). Miriam's punishment was to be excluded from the camp of the Israelites for seven long days.

Miriam and Aaron's problem was speaking in the wrong voice or against the will of God, and temporarily losing their voice as a result. We've all spoken in the wrong voice at some point, but when God's appointed authority is challenged, that is serious and dangerous speech.

When leaders make the wrong choices or sin, they lose their voice—or they should. King Saul lost his voice of authority with his servants. When Saul told his bodyguards to kill Abimelech the priest, they refused. An amazing incident! Saul's own army refused to obey him. *"The king's officials were not willing to raise a hand to strike the priests of the Lord"* (First Samuel 22:17). He lost his authority because of his anger, jealousy and hatred toward David.

As I study these biblical examples and recall the downfall of some TV evangelists and other prominent pastors, a holy fear comes over me. *I don't want to lose my voice.*

Like any Christian leader, I have a lot to lose if I am disobedient to my calling. I have a lot of different voices: as a husband, father, grandfather, pastor, preacher, public speaker, and currently, as a para-church leader. Yes, I have a lot to lose if I lose my voice.

When Job defended himself, he talked about the blessing of having a strong voice. He said that when he spoke, *"...the young stepped aside when they saw me, and even the aged rose in respect to my coming. The princes stood in silence and put their hands over their mouths. The highest officials of the city stood quietly, holding their tongues in respect"* (Job 29:8-10). That is some respect! That is the kind of voice all leaders need.

Peter lost his voice when he denied the Lord. After the resurrection, Peter and six other disciples returned to the very life they had left behind, as fishermen (See John 21). As Jesus revealed Himself to them again, Peter had a second call to follow the Messiah. The next time we read about Peter and the disciples, they were standing all together on the day of Pentecost, addressing throngs of people. *"Then Peter stood up with the Eleven, raised his voice and addressed the crowd"* (Acts 2:14).

A Lost Voice Can Be Reclaimed!

Elijah ran from Jezebel and hid in the wilderness, fearing for his life, and he lost his voice. The prophet was burned out! The Lord understood Elijah's weariness in well doing and ministered to his physical and spiritual needs (See First Kings 19). His ministry and voice were restored and continued until the mantle was passed on to Elisha.

My favorite account of a lost and regained voice is Zechariah, the faithful priest serving in the temple. One day, an angel appeared to him at the right side of the altar and told him that his prayers had been answered and Elizabeth, his wife, would bear a son (See Luke 1:11-17).

Did you ever pray for something and when the answer came, or was about to come, you doubted? If so, you can lose your voice for such unbelief. Zechariah did! He questioned the angel: *"How can I be sure of this? I am an old man and my wife well along in years?"* (Luke 1:18) It was no ordinary angel who brought this word regarding the birth of John the Baptist. It was the archangel Gabriel. God sent his top messenger to make this announcement of the announcer to come. Zechariah was unwilling to believe it. For this, he lost his voice for nine months!

The good news is that lost voices can be regained! When it was time to name the baby, the relatives wanted to follow tradition and give Elizabeth's child a traditional family name, but she insisted that his name must be John. The family was shocked, *"'What?' they exclaimed. 'There is no one in all your family by that name.' So they used gestures to ask the baby's father what he wanted to name him. He motioned for a writing tablet, and to everyone's surprise, he wrote, 'His name is John.' Instantly Zechariah could speak again, and he began praising God"* (Luke 1:59-64).

When Jesus went into the village of Nain, He encountered a funeral procession. A young lad, the only son of a widow, had died. Jesus stopped the crowd of mourners and touched the coffin. The boy sat up, being brought back to life. Luke 7:15 says that the lad began to speak. Although this is not a parable, but a real miracle, it can also be a spiritual type. Dead people don't speak. What is true in the natural is true in the spiritual. With spiritual life comes the power of voice.

I have seen pastors, preachers, deacons, lay persons, worship leaders and teachers lose their voice either because of sin or other negative issues. However, some have reclaimed an anointed voice. King David did. Elijah did. Moses did after forty years in the wilderness, and so did a priest named Zechariah.

14
STAYING OUT FRONT

*When you see the Ark of the Covenant and
the priests who are carrying it, you are to
move out from your position and follow it*
(Joshua 3:3).

A pastor once said to me in jest, "There goes my people. I must catch up to them, for I am their leader." It seems elementary to say that a leader needs to stay out in front of the people he or she leads. That should be an obvious, essential leadership quality.

Now, I am open to new ideas, and I am well aware that I do not always have the answers to every problem facing the ministry or the church. But when it comes to the overall direction of where we need to go, I need to have a vision for the future and implement the steps to get us there. I need to be out front. It is scary sometimes to be out front leading, especially when the fog of circumstances comes in unrelentingly. Yet, if I have to remind people that I am in charge and the leader, it is a sign of insecurity.

Staying out front involves at least three important things:

1. The leader must have the ability to hear the voice of God regarding the direction the ministry is to go in.

"As soon as the priests carrying the ark reached the Jordan and their feet touched the water's edge, the

water from upstream stopped flowing" (Joshua 3:3). The priests who led the congregation across the Jordan, *"stood firm in the middle of the Jordan, while all Israel passed by until the whole nation had completed the crossing on dry ground"* (Joshua 3:17).

People want to be led. They will follow leaders, even when it means taking risks of faith, standing firm in the vision put forth under the anointing of the Holy Spirit. Robert E. Lee was a strong leader who understood the power of leadership. He wrote, *"You must be careful how you walk, and where you go, for there are those following you who will set their foot where yours are set."*[1] This is exactly what Israel's crossing of the Jordan River into the Promised Land is a picture of.

2. The leader must make right judgments.

One of the most important decisions I can make is selecting the right people to be, as the expression goes, "on the bus with me." I have to be the driver and make right judgments of those who will join the journey "for the long haul" and those who may be "short-termers." It is the Holy Spirit who calls people and brings them to my attention, but I have to discern and confirm that it is God's call for them to be on our ministry's bus. If we are not a right fit for one another, it will frustrate their ministry as well as ours.

My second greatest challenge in making judgment calls is deciding who should be "under-shepherds" leading others in the church body. In other words, who do I choose to be out front with me to lead the ministry team to our destination?

One of the most important tasks Jesus had in the beginning of His ministry was choosing His disciples. He saw them not for just what they were when He first called them, but for their future potential. For example, Jesus said to the disciple we know as Peter, *"You are Simon, son of John. You will be called Cephas [which when translated is Peter]"* (John 1:42). Note the vision Jesus had for Peter when he said, *"You are...you will be."* A good leader sees the potential of what others can become in time. Rightly choosing the members of your team is one of the most important judgment calls for a pastor/leader. And just as Jesus went to His Father in prayer for all of His decisions, we need to do the same so that we will be led to make the right choices.

3. The leader must diffuse potential obstacles in carrying out a vision.

I could write an entire book on the vital need for a leader to stay out in front to see impending problems, and put out potentially dangerous fires before they cause irreparable damage. This includes keeping a spirit of unity between the leader and those serving under him or her. It also includes addressing developing jealousies, territorialism, wounded egos, and other possible causes of strife among team members.

I recall a new leader coming to me after having been in our ministry about a month. He said, "You know, I'm seeing a lot of problems that you may not be aware of, and I need to bring these things to your attention." He proceeded to bring out a laundry list of problems he perceived.

I listened politely, then smiled and said, "It's far worse than what you have shared! I've been here for years, and I know things we're dealing with that you haven't even seen yet! What you're seeing is just some of our problems." Then I carefully explained to him how such problems are inherent when working with the type of hurting people we minister to, and that our workers are dedicated, but not perfect.

"My job," I explained, "is to minimize these problems and stay out ahead of them so we can put out a small fire before it becomes a big one and someone gets burnt."

Peter had to address the Jewish believers in Acts, chapter 11 when he was criticized for going into a house of uncircumcised men to eat with them. Peter's strong defense satisfied their objections (See Acts 11:1-18). He was staying ahead of the problem by helping to clarify an issue that could have been divisive to the fledgling church.

Putting your feet first in the water can be scary and risk-taking. Leaders are to set the example in matters of faith. A boat is safe in a harbor, but that's not the purpose of a boat. We will always be out front in leading souls to Christ and leading a church or para-church if we do as Joshua did: *"Joshua said to the Israelites, 'Come here and listen to the words of the Lord your God'"* (Joshua 3:9, NIV). Joshua heard from the Lord and any man or woman of God who does so, will always be out front in leadership because he or she allows the Lord to be first and foremost in their lives.

When speaking to young ministers on how to be successful in planting a church, Charles Spurgeon said:

> *Preach your Bible and preach as you find it in the simplicity of the language. Begin to tell people what you have felt in your own heart, and beg the Holy Spirit to make your heart as hot as a furnace for zeal.*

> *Then go out and talk to the people. Speak*
> *to them like their brother. Be a man among*
> *men. Tell them what you have felt and*
> *know, and tell it heartily with a good, bold*
> *face.*[2]

True leadership requires staying out in front, sharing the vision, solving problems, and hearing the voice of God to know what word to share with the church or ministry.

15

THE USE AND MISUSE OF INFORMATION

It is the glory of God to conceal a matter;
to search out a matter is the glory of kings
(Proverbs 25:2, NIV).

A leader often has privileged information and has to be spiritually sensitive as to with whom and when it should be shared. Information can be a blessing or a curse, and the wise use of it is vital in any church, organization or ministry. Over the years, I have acquired sensitive knowledge and information concerning some individuals that will go to the grave with me.

On a regular basis, I am faced with the decision of whether to share certain information with my staff and coworkers in ministry. Sensitive information can be either gossip or gospel. It can be instructive or destructive. Some people collect bad information like garbage, and then they like to throw it around. Many a pastor, leader or worker has been deeply hurt when information that should have been deleted (from our memory computer) or kept private, was instead passed along to others. We should never forget that information that is filtered through others and then passed along is often tainted, distorted, or an outright falsehood.

During the Cold War, when negotiating nuclear weapons treaties with the Soviet Union, President Ronald Regan had an expression that ought to be followed by churches and ministries: *Trust, but verify.*

A leader's source of information is not always accurate. I have mistakenly taken action that turned out to be the wrong decision because I trusted the source of the information, but did not verify it with another source. Proverbs 15:22 reminds us that, *"In the multitude of counselors there is wisdom,"* and usually better information, as well!

Sharing the Vision

I also have found that sharing a vision for the ministry to the wrong person can be either misunderstood or too overwhelming. Visionaries tend to think everyone should be just as enthusiastic about their vision as they are. Would you tell an eight or ten-year-old what you might tell an adult? Of course not. The same holds true for spiritual children—they may be unable to understand future plans and visions. Ultimately, the vision might involve them, but they don't need to know about it until the steps are implemented to work the vision.

In the book of Genesis, we have the story of Joseph and the mistakes he made sharing his dreams with his brothers before the time was right. *"Joseph had a dream, and when he told it to his brothers, they hated him all the more"* (Genesis 37:5).

When the children of Israel marched around Jericho, they were given instructions on a need-to-know basis. Joshua told them on day one of the march, *"Do not give a war cry, do not raise your voices; do not say a word until the day I tell you to shout. Then Shout!"* (Joshua 6:10) I have seen too much shouting too soon in Gospel work and in spiritual warfare. As a result, information can leak out before the right time and things can go wrong; someone may even try to sabotage the plan.

Information is knowledge and knowledge is power. It can bring about much good, or it can bring evil. Unverified information can be gossip, and sadly, some people thrive on gossip. And gossip is not always incorrect. There's a lot of truthful information that simply should not be passed around. Often, the difference between gossip and news is whether you hear it or tell it!

"The things that go in one ear and out the other do not hurt as much as the things that go in one ear, get mixed up, and then slip out of the mouth."[1] Beth Moore writes in *Breaking Free,* "Out of the overflow of a changed heart, the mouth most beautifully speaks."[2]

Why Didn't Someone Tell Me?

Another aspect of information is the necessity of dispensing right information to the right persons. Withholding information can be as harmful as sharing the wrong information and gossiping. Abraham withheld information that Sarah was his wife and God had to tell Abimelech in a dream not to touch her (See Genesis 20).

"Why didn't someone tell me?" is a frequent thought that runs through my mind, especially when I had to deal with a difficult situation and I did not have all the information on hand to make a timely and accurate decision. Information withheld by lay people and ministry staff can blindside a leader, even when it is done innocently.

In the Old Testament, young Samuel was tested early on in his calling. The Lord told him something that *"...will make the ears of everyone who hears of it tingle"* (See First Samuel 3:11-21, NIV). This had to do with God's judgment coming upon Eli the priest, because he did not discipline his sons for treating the temple sacrifices and offerings with contempt (See First Samuel 2:12-26).

Later, when Eli realized the Word of the Lord had come to young Samuel, he asked him to share it. *"So Samuel told him everything, hiding nothing from him. Then Eli said, 'He is the LORD; let him do what is good in his eyes'"* (First Samuel 3:18, NIV). It took courage for Samuel to share such a heavy message with his spiritual leader, and it took discipline to withhold it until the time was right.

Some people thrive on having certain knowledge others do not have and they proudly flaunt it; perhaps sharing some tidbits, but then, withholding other information. Still others babble everything they know for the purpose of making themselves feel important. *"Wise people treasure knowledge, but the babbling of a fool invites trouble"* (Proverbs 10:14). *"Those who feel they know the most, often know the least"* (Croft Pentz).[3]

There is an ancient saying: *"Have you heard a word against your neighbor? Let it die within you, trusting it will not burst you."* Those are wise words to adhere to! Some things should be pondered in our hearts and minds before sharing. *"Mary quietly treasured these things in her heart and thought about them often"* (Luke 2:19). Jesus withheld information from His disciples until they were ready to handle it. "There is so much more I want to tell you, but you can't bear it now" (John 16:12).

Following Christ's Example

Leaders should follow Christ's example in how He shared and communicated with His disciples. God is too good to give us answers to some prayers we pray because we are not prepared to handle such blessings. God is also too good to give us knowledge that is too high for us, and especially if such knowledge would cause us either fear or pride (See Psalm 139:6).

When sharing vision, it is not good to blow an uncertain trumpet, but it's also not good to blow it too soon. Wait until your people have fallen in line. The successful leader is one who makes the right move at the right moment with the right motive, and with having shared the right information in the process. And the Christian leader has a true advantage when the Holy Spirit is guiding him, because His timing is perfect!

Proverbs 25 gives some practical instruction on the use and misuse of information. *"It is the glory of God to conceal a matter"* (v. 2). Don't be hasty in making judgments based on information that has not been verified: *"Go not forth hastily to strive, lest thou know not what to do in the end thereof, when thy neighbor hath put you to shame"* (vs. 7-8, KJV). Don't betray a neighbor with misinformation (See vs. 9-10, 18). *"A word aptly spoken is like apples of gold in settings of silver"* (v. 11).

The last word on this I'd like to mention is that we must distinguish between knowledge and information that is God's Word, and what is man's word, and never confuse the two. I assume the reader understands that "information" in this chapter deals with the everyday type of communication between leaders and those being led. Sometimes new or young converts think a leader's word is infallible and always comes directly from God. But that is simply not so!

Paul the Apostle clearly distinguished between his word and God's Word on the matter of whether one should marry or not. He said regarding marriage,

"I wish that all men were as I am." But he prefaced it by saying, *"I speak this by permission, and not of commandment"* (1 Corinthians 7:6-7, KJV).

Many a church member or ministry worker has been confused by a pastor or leader's misuse of information, and vice versa. On the other hand, Paul the Apostle's testimony regarding Philemon is the model to follow. *"The communication of thy faith may become effective by the acknowledging of every good thing that is in you in Christ Jesus"* (Philemon 6, KJV).

A word spoken in due season, how good it is (Proverbs 15:23, NKJV).

16

WAFFLING ON NO

*Simply let your "Yes" be "Yes"
and your "No" be "No." Anything
beyond this comes from the evil one*
(Matthew 5:37, NIV; See also James 5:12).

A waffle can be a breakfast food or an uncertain word; the former tastes good and the latter can leave a very bad taste in one's mind. The waffle I speak of is defined as being indecisive and vague in speech. Waffling on "no" is when we say yes and not mean it, or say no and not mean that either. Leaders who waffle quickly lose credibility. Jesus uses pretty strong language about keeping our word. He was talking about following through on our vows. In those days, one's word was equivalent to an agreement drawn up by a lawyer and recorded in a court of law.

The principle applies today for each of us, but leaders especially must remain firm to their word and their promises. Many a church member or worker in a ministry has been disappointed by a leader who did not keep his word. I have also been guilty of disappointing people by not keeping my word. My mistake sometimes was to give a thoughtless yes or no to a matter, only to find out that the person I spoke to took my word at face value. (How dare they!) Then later, when I did think it through and decided the opposite decision would really be best, the person who heard me was left disappointed and confused. If this becomes a pattern in a leader, the entire organization can find itself in chaos. When I make this mistake, it really causes confusion. When leaders constantly make this mistake, it will surely result in a loss of credibility.

I have regretted many a yes decision over the course of my life and ministry. I should have heeded James 1:19: *"My dear brothers, take note of this; everyone should be quick to listen, slow to speak, and slow to anger."*

A habitual "yes" person may have the problem of wanting to be a people-pleaser. Good leaders cannot and do not try to please everyone.

Some leaders tend to put off hard decisions— whether the decision needs to be in the affirmative or negative. I can be very impatient in handling day-to-day matters, but patient to a fault when having to make decisions that are difficult to make. I find it much easier now that I'm in my later years to say yes to people and decisions that need to be made in respect to ministry and organizational matters, but I find it harder to say no. In certain cultures, if you do not say "No" outright it is taken as a yes. If you say, "I'll pray about it," or "I'll look into the matter," or anything else other than a definite "No," it is interpreted as a yes.

When I do think through and pray through an important decision, I have no trouble letting my "yes" be yes or my "no" be no. Pastors and leaders make mistakes when church members or staff catch them on the fly, and a quick response is given that has not been thought through. Proverbs 10:19 says, *"He who holds his tongue is wise."*

When it comes to matters of good and evil, righteousness and unrighteousness, there can be no waffling. A "yes" to Christ and the Word of God means a "no" to the world, the flesh and the devil. But in other non-biblical matters, knowing whether to answer yes or no can be a challenge.

Some Famous No Answers in the Bible

1. Joseph's "no" when being seduced by Potiphar's wife. *"How could I ever do such a wicked thing? It would be a great sin against God"* (Genesis 39:9).

Seduction does not just come by sexual advances. Leaders can be seduced by power, position, money and other things. Matthew Henry wrote, *"Those that would not eat the forbidden fruit must not come near the forbidden tree."*[1]

2. Elisha's "no" when offered a gift by Naaman after his healing. *"Now please accept my gifts. But Elisha replied, 'As surely as the Lord lives, whom I serve, I will not accept any gifts.' And though Naaman urged him to take the gifts, Elisha refused"* (Second Kings 5:15-16).

Elisha's refusal to take a gift from the commander of a foreign army who had been cleansed of his leprosy was the right thing to do, so as to demonstrate that God's favors have no price to them. A. W. Tozer writes, *"The world says, 'In everything by money,' but the church should say, 'In everything by prayer'"*[2] (See Philippians 4:6).

3. Queen Vashti's "no" when asked to parade her beauty before King Xerxes' military leaders at their banquet. *"She refused to come. This made the king furious, and he burned with anger"* (Esther 1:11-12).

This act of defiance caused uproar among the King's men as they feared a women's movement might threaten their male control, and Vashti was banished from the presence of the King. Yet, Vashti's courage in standing up to the King resulted in Esther replacing her in the divine providence of God. Esther's uncle Mordecai also spoke a famous biblical "no" when he refused to bow down before Haman, an official of the King. This decision ultimately led to the near destruction, but later deliverance of the Jews.

There are times for momentous, history-making "no's" and times for simple "no's" in everyday situations and communications. I have seen when a straightforward no could have saved trouble within families, ministries and churches. *"The devil may send the package, but I'm responsible for signing for it."*[3]

The Yes Trap

I caused my family to suffer in the earlier days of my ministry because I rarely refused to say no to an invitation to preach. I recall my father telling me to never say no to an opportunity in the pulpit. As a result, I often took time away from my family when I should not have done so. It didn't occur to me at the time that my father's invitations to speak were primarily local and regional, while mine were national and international, requiring much more time away from home.

One leader confided in me that he ran himself ragged saying yes to everyone and everything because, "I wanted people to accept me. I was driven by a desire for approval and I thought by accepting any and all invitations, I would be loved by everyone. I wanted to please! The truth is, I was taken advantage of by others."

I still fall into the "yes" trap at times. For me, the hardest time to say no is when someone is seeking an open door to ministry and they ask me for help. I love to empower others for ministry. However, decisions must not be made emotionally, based on need (either the person's need to serve or my need to meet a need), or any consideration other than the will of God. I get several letters a month from someone who wants to serve in the ministry I lead, or they ask me if I know of positions open where they can serve. I must carefully and prayerfully take these before the Lord before giving any answers.

Recently, a pastor came to my attention at the very moment we had a need for his gifts, experience and talents. I said to him, "This is a no-brainer. You're available. You're looking to use your gifts somewhere. We have a need—it's a perfect match." Saying yes was easy in this case. In most other cases, a no is required. I rest in knowing that it is God, not me, who opens and closes doors.

When we are walking in the Spirit, letting our yes be yes and our no be no is not a difficult task. Paul wanted to go to Asia to preach, but instead went somewhere else *"...because the Holy Spirit had told them not to go into the province of Asia at that time."* Then they tried to go to the province of Bithynia and *"...again the Spirit of Jesus did not let them go"* (Acts 16:6-8).

The Holy Spirit is an expert at knowing when to say yes and when to say no. We need to rest in His leading to help us make those decisions.

17
LESSONS FROM ITTAI AND SHIMEI DURING KING DAVID'S TIME

Then the king turned to Ittai, the captain of the Gittites, and asked, "Why are you coming with us? Go on back to King Absalom, for you are a guest in Israel, a foreigner in exile."

It was Shimei son of Gera, from the same clan as Saul's family. He threw stones at the king (Second Samuel 15:19; 16:5-6).

In case you are not familiar with Ittai and Shimei, let me introduce you to Mr. Loyalty and Mr. Disloyalty; the latter deserves an Academy Award in mockery of a public figure. In Second Samuel chapters 15 and 16, we find a great example of loyalty and respect and disloyalty and disrespect towards leadership.

It was during the time that King David fled Jerusalem because his son Absalom was attempting to overthrow his father's kingship. So David fled the city, along with his household and his bodyguards, including six hundred Gittites, foreign soldiers employed to guard the king and his palace. The captain of these soldiers was a man named Ittai. David urged him to *"...go on back to King Absalom, for you are a guest in Israel, a foreigner in exile"* (Second Samuel 15:17-20).

Though they had just arrived the day before to protect King David, Ittai responded in a manner similar to when Ruth declared her loyalty to Naomi. Ittai said, *"I vow by the Lord and by your own life that*

I will go wherever my lord the King goes, no matter what happens—whether it means life or death" (Second Samuel 15:21).

Every leader needs such devotion. I could make a long list of individuals who have been an "Ittai" to me over the years. Without them, I could never carry on the work God has given me to do. I will take one loyal, faithful servant over 10 talented workers who do not have the gift of servanthood and faithfulness. Paul the Apostle had such faithful servants and mentions several of them, including Tychicus (Ephesians 6:21) and Epaphas (Colossians 1:7). One cannot be faithful to the Lord without also being faithful to those you serve under.

At this time, when David was facing a challenge to his leadership and when his own safety was in question, God gave him an Ittai. We all need such individuals at strategic times in our lives. Loyalty to Jesus Christ must always be first, and out of this will come a godly loyalty to others. Carter Conlin, (Pastor of Times Square Church in Manhattan, New York) stated in a sermon, *"Our commitment to others will never exceed our commitment to God."*

In contrast to Ittai is Shimei. During the same period of Ittai's allegiance to David, a former loyalist to King Saul named Shimei sees David and his people passing by his village and makes a scene mocking him.

> *He threw stones at the king and the king's officers and all the mighty warriors who surrounded him. "Get out of here, you murderer, you scoundrel!" he shouted at David. "The LORD is paying you back for all the bloodshed in Saul's clan. You stole his throne, and now the LORD has given it to*

your son Absalom. At last you will taste some of your own medicine, for you are a murderer!" (Second Samuel 16: 5-8)

What would I have done if I was David? How might you have reacted? Probably in a more civil manner than David's right hand man Abishai wanted to do, requesting to cut off Shimei's head (Second Samuel 16:9). David's response is a lesson in discipline, patience and self-control. He took the abuse, knowing it was allowed by a sovereign God as a test to his own character. David assured his men that God was allowing it and *"...will bless me because of these curses"* (Second Samuel 16:12).

Thankfully, I have had many more Ittais serve me than I have had Shimeis attack me; though I have had my share of the latter. I have not always acted in the godly manner that David did when shown such utter disrespect. David kept his head, while others wanted to have his attacker's head roll.

Not only did Shimei curse the king, he continued to do so as David and his company fled from Jerusalem. Second Samuel 16:13-14 says, *"So David and his men continued down the road, and Shimei kept pace with them on a nearby hillside, cursing as he went and throwing stones at David and tossing dust into the air. The king and all who were with him grew weary along the way, so they rested when they reached the Jordan River."*

I assume David was weary from the physical journey, as well as the emotional reaction to the relentless scorn he had to endure from Shimei. It was bad enough that Absalom was trying to take his throne; an angry member of Saul's family was attacking David's reputation, as well. Nevertheless, David left Shimei's outcome in the hands of God.

"No cruelty, no crime, no injustice escapes the attention of God" (Kay Arthur).[1]

The end of the story for Shimei came much later under Solomon's reign. David gave his final words to his son Solomon. He asked the new King to arrange a bloody death for Shimei. Justice was finally done (See First Kings 2:8-9).

God takes care of the Shimeis in life. Jesus said, *"But I say, Love your enemies! Pray for those that persecute you"* (Matthew 5:44).

18

NO SWEAT

Apart from Me you can do nothing (John 15:5).

There was an expression I don't often hear today: whenever someone was asked to take on a difficult challenge, they might brag and say, "No sweat." Or someone might say, "It's a piece of cake" and mean the same thing—an expression of a *can-do* attitude.

In the Old Testament, the Levitical priesthood was not allowed to perspire when serving in the Tabernacle or Temple. They were not allowed to sweat! Here is the regulation and commandment regarding this from Ezekiel 44:17-18:

> *When they enter the gateway to the courtyard they must wear only linen clothing. They must wear no wool while on duty in the inner courtyard or in the Temple itself. They must wear linen turbans and linen undergarments. They must not wear anything that would cause them to perspire.* (The latter is translated *"sweat"* in the King James Version.)

Why no sweat? What is the meaning of this? Sweat represents the flesh! God's work must be done not *"...by force nor by [human] strength, but by my Spirit, says the Lord Almighty"* (Zechariah 4:6, NIV). This prophecy was that Zerubbabel was to lay the foundation stone for the rebuilt Temple in Jerusalem, and that the people of God needed to know it was the Lord's doing.

This principle is carried throughout Scripture: that it is not by human ability, intelligence or power that the work of God is to be accomplished, but by reliance on the power of God through the Holy Spirit. *"Unless the Lord build the house, they labor in vain that build it"* (Psalm 127:1). Man likes to build! Building takes planning, execution, labor, sweat—lots of human sweat. Building God's kingdom ought to be done with the Holy Spirit working in and through us, without thinking that the results depend on our natural and human efforts. There is too much sweat in kingdom work today.

Spiritual Inventory

At the end of each year, as New Year's Day approaches, I try to take a spiritual inventory. One year, not so long ago, my prayer to the Lord was, *"Lord, I want to work less and accomplish more."* I sometimes think that God's work depends more on me than on God. I do not consciously operate like this, but by my workaholic habits it turns out this way. I must continually repent and quote to myself Jesus' words to His disciples, *"Apart from Me you can do nothing"* (John 15:5).

No one was a harder worker than the Apostle Paul. At times, he worked to exhaustion (2 Corinthians 6:5), and he lived with weariness and pain and sleepless nights. And besides that, he had the daily care of many churches (See 2 Corinthians 11:27, 28).

David Platt, in his book, *Radical* focuses on *"taking back your faith from the American Dream."* He writes the following:

The problem for us is that in our culture we are tempted at every turn to trust in our own power instead [of God's]. The dangerous assumption we can unknowingly accept in the American dream is that our greatest asset is our own ability. The American dream prizes what people can accomplish when they believe in themselves, and we are drawn toward such thinking. But the Gospel has different priorities. The Gospel beckons us to die to ourselves and to believe in God and to trust in His power. In the Gospel, God confronts us with our utter inability to accomplish anything of value apart from Him. This is what Jesus meant when He said, 'I am the vine; you are the branches. If a man remains in me and I in him, he will bear much fruit; apart from me you can do nothing.' ...the goal of the American dream is to make much of us; the goal of the Gospel is to make much of God."[1]

For many people, sweat becomes a source of pride to be worn like an expensive cologne; when in fact it can be an offensive odor in the nostrils of God: *"Not of works, lest any man should boast!"* (Ephesians 2:9, KJV)

Today, many churches and ministries are run like corporations led by CEO's. This is both good and bad. All ministries should be conducted with sound business principles, with integrity, discipline, and productivity. This is the good part. But when the church becomes entertainment, (the hyping of special events to keep the crowds coming and catering to the congregation as if they are consumers who, if not satisfied, will go shopping at another Gospel mall) this is "flesh" and not Spirit.

Once, Christians realized that the kingdom of God was built by those who were seen as foolish in the eyes of the world. Now, the church is often embarrassed to be seen as weak. But *"the weakness of God is stronger than man's strength"* (1 Corinthians 1:25).

My brother David wrote a bestselling book in the 1960's entitled, *The Cross and the Switchblade.* The book tells the story of how Teen Challenge came into being and how drug addicts were cured when they had a personal encounter with Jesus Christ. In addition, my brother and I (in the formation of this ministry) discovered that when the former addicts were baptized in the Holy Spirit, they were (and are still today) better able to stay free from their life-controlling problems.

As our team of evangelists and prayer warriors ventured out to reach the gangs and later the drug addicts for Christ, I recall that David would quote 1 Corinthians over and over again. My brother was certain that God chose *"...the foolish things of the world"* (meaning us) *"to confound the wise,"* (See 1 Corinthians 1:25-28) as He used us to reach those in bondage. We knew we could take no credit for the miracle of the changed lives of gang members, drug addicts and alcoholics. We were a bunch of nobodies, but we were Spirit-filled! It was the Lord building the house—the ministry. At the end of the day, our boasting had to be in the Lord (See 1 Corinthians 1:29, 31). The same is true today at Brooklyn Teen Challenge—the flagship center. E. M. Bounds wrote: *"The Holy Spirit does not flow through methods, but through men."*[2] When we sweat, strive, and trust in our own methods to solve human problems and bondages, we wear ourselves out and see little fruit for such efforts. The old saying remains true, *"On one hand, we must exercise faith as if everything depended on God; while at the same time, work as if everything depends on us!*[3]" Whenever the latter takes over the former, we are crushed beneath our own striving.

PART THREE
Advice to Future Leaders

19
CALLING AND ENABLING

We constantly pray for you, that our God may count you worthy of his calling, and that by his power he may fulfill every good purpose of yours and every act prompted by your faith (2 Thessalonians 1:12, NIV).

I was taught as a young aspiring preacher that what God *called* me to do He would *enable* me to do. Billy Graham has said, "God never calls a person [into His service] without equipping him. I know that from experience."[1] I agree with Dr. Graham, but for a long time my question was, "What exactly is my calling?" Yes, I knew I was to enter the ministry, but in what capacity? Was I to be a pastor, an evangelist, a missionary?

I tried my best to become a foreign missionary. They were the superstars in my mind who were definitely fulfilling God's call. Next were evangelists, followed by pastors. I did not know what a para-church ministry was at the time, so I didn't even consider it. During Bible College, I joined the African Prayer Band to see if I had a call to Africa! But I quickly learned that was my plan, and not God's.

Even after being in Teen Challenge for some years, conducting street evangelism, preaching, fundraising, administrative work (even helping my brother produce a TV documentary), I still did not know exactly what ministry I was called to fulfill. Then, I began a study on the spiritual gifts. Through that study, the Lord showed me that my primary gift was to pastor or shepherd His people, with secondary complementary gifts of administration and wisdom. This led to the discovery that what God was enabling me to do was actually defining my calling.

Discover Your Gifting

At times in ministry, I am called to do the work of an evangelist, but I know it is not my primary gift. So, if I struggle when preaching evangelistically, I do not get discouraged. I leave the results in the Lord's hands. When I feel led to speak a prophetic message, I do so out of obedience to the leading of the Holy Spirit; yet I know such messages are the exception and not the norm for me.

For a time, I questioned my pastoral gift because I began my ministry in a para-church organization, not as the pastor of a local congregation. Was I out of the will of God? Then, one day a Bible college friend came by Teen Challenge and, in the course of showing him through our ministry, he asked me a question. "What is the difference between what I do as a pastor and what you do here ministering to gangs, drug addicts and alcoholics?"

The question really made me think. It took me a while to come up with the answer. Finally, I said, "Well, when you preach on Sunday morning and give the benediction, you and your congregation go home. When we pray the benediction here at Teen Challenge, we are already home. I live most of the time with my congregation." In other words, I began to see that there was no difference between being a pastor of a traditional congregation and working at Teen Challenge. I was still a pastor, one who would come alongside the sheep to lead, guide, and train them. I get to pastor all day long! My church, my congregants, just all happened to have a life-controlling problem, an addiction. I was secure in my *calling,* doing what God was *enabling* me to do.

God's power enables us to do what we're called to do. 2 Thessalonians 1:12 (NIV) says, *"That our God may count you worthy of his calling, and that by his power he may fulfill every good purpose of yours."* 2 Thessalonians 5:24 says, *"The one who calls you is faithful, and he will do it."* As many ministers of the Gospel have noted, "God doesn't call people who are qualified. He calls people who are willing, and He qualifies them!"

When I interview someone who wants to work at Teen Challenge, I try to find out what is their God-given enabling. I do this by asking what gives them the greatest joy in service or ministry. If it is soul winning, I know they may not have the *enabling* to work close with a new convert in helping them grow spiritually, but they will be *able* to reach the unsaved who come to the ministry for help.

Once, when teaching on spiritual gifts, I asked the class how many knew what their gift was and a young man spoke up and said he believed he had the gift of healing. I asked if anyone had been healed when he prayed for them. He said "No." I answered him clearly, "Then you don't have the gift of healing."

My father often quoted and taught me that, *"A man's gift makes room for him, and brings him before great men"* (Proverbs 18:16).

Your Greatest Fulfillment

I believe a person finds their greatest fulfillment when they can exercise their enabling gift. What I call an enabling gift is also called by some, *our motivational gift.* It is what strongly motivates us to do the work of the Lord in the Body of Christ. 1 Peter 4:10 states,

"God has given each of you a gift from His great variety of spiritual gifts. Use them well to serve one another."

> *Most Christians are already using their spiritual gifts to one degree or another, even though they have not identified them. But they could use them more effectively, more frequently, more decisively and more strategically if they became more consciously aware of what spiritual gifts they possessed. In other words, a better knowledge of our gifts will help us serve others better* (J. E. O'Day).[2]

I have seen ministers, church and para-church workers spending years fulfilling someone else's counsel of how they should serve. They may have a measure of success in what they're doing, but if they find God's enabling gift, they will be much more successful and satisfied in their serving.

In the early days of Teen Challenge, one of our board members, Paul, and his wife, Sonya, would entertain some VIPs that came to visit our ministry. On one occasion I said to Sonya, "Do you know you have a very special gift that God has given you?" She looked at me, puzzled. "Yes, you have a biblical gift. Both you and your husband (a policeman) have the gift of hospitality." She smiled and said, "No one has ever said that to me." She was simply doing what came naturally to her, but in fact it was much more than that. She and her husband were expressing their God-given *enabling* gift of hospitality. 1 Peter 4:9-10 mentions the need for hospitality in the church, followed by these words from the Apostle Peter: *"Each one should use whatever gift he has received to serve others, faithfully administering God's grace in various ways."*

Sometimes we make the gifts too mysterious or too selective. The gifts of hospitality, helps and giving often go unnoticed in the body of Christ, both by the ones having the gifts and those who are blessed by them. 1 Corinthians 7:7 reminds us that, *"Each man has his own gift from God; one has this gift, another has that."* The footnotes from the *Life in the Spirit Bible* refer to the spiritual gifts as grace gifts that "involve both an inward motivation and the power to perform ministry (i.e., actualized enablement)." They are given to strengthen the church and those in need of spiritual help.

> *There are people whose lives are waiting to be affected by what God has placed within you. So evaluate yourself. Define and refine your gifts, talents and strengths. Choose today to look for opportunities to exercise your unique, God-endowed, God-ordained gifts and calling* (John Mason).[3]

20
LISTENING

My dear brothers, take note of this:
Everyone should be quick to listen,
slow to speak and slow to become angry
(James 1:19, NIV).

I almost entitled this book, *Things They Never Taught Me in Bible College.* Another thing I did not learn early on in my ministry is the importance of being a patient listener, or what some call *the art of listening.* Larry King, who retired from CNN in 2011 after having conducted some 40,000 interviews in his lifetime on radio and TV said, *"I never learned anything while I was talking."*[1] What an excellent quote to remember!

My wife says I don't listen to her. At least I think that's what she says. Seriously, beginning with my wife and children, I have not always been a good listener. The reason for this was because I was often too preoccupied with my own thoughts, needs, and plans. Selfishness and self-centeredness are at the root of being a poor or a non-listener. People, generally, are not good listeners. They are too preoccupied with themselves. But for leaders, listening is essential. My wife tells me I should not only listen when others speak to me, but I should *appear* to be listening, as well. I had an office person who would never look me in the eye when she spoke to me. She did not last long.

There are three levels of listening: (1) Listen to what is being said. (2) Listen to what is not being said. (3) Listen to what a person seems unable to say.

Peter Drucker, famous management consultant and author, is often quoted, *"The most important thing in communication is to hear what isn't being said."*[2] Long ago a teacher told us that our class would be graded not only on the answers we gave on tests and quizzes, but on the questions we asked in class. The questions, she explained, would let her know how well we were listening! What a wise woman.

Be Quick to Listen

Too often we quit listening before the other person quits talking. We are more interested in what we have to say than in hearing the other person out. However, listen we must! Spouses with their mate! Parents with children! Children with parents—at any age! Pastors and leaders with our hired staff, our volunteers and the least among us.

My father was loved by his congregation because he was a good listener, especially to those people he called "birds with a broken wing," people others often paid very little attention to.

In counseling others, I have often been quick to cut a person off and give advice when I don't have all the facts. This is a clear violation of Scripture. Sometimes I have ended up trying to answer questions that weren't even being asked. In the New English Bible, Proverbs 18:13 says, *"To answer a question before you have heard it out, is both stupid and insulting."* Ouch!

In his epistle, James admonishes, *"Everyone should be quick to listen, slow to speak"* (1:19). I know someone who always wants to finish my sentences for me. It's very annoying!

Perhaps ministry schools need seminars or even an entire class purely on the subject of LISTENING! I am told that on Facebook or when texting, that using capital letters is the equivalent of shouting. The caps are intended!

In their book, *God is in the Small Stuff,* authors Bruce Bickel and Stan Jantz write that, *"Communication is more than talking"*[3] and list the following excellent points:

- *"Listen with your eyes as well as your ears."*
- *"No one will accuse you of being a boring conversationalist if you let people talk about themselves."*
- *"You learn more by listening. You already know what you would say."*
- *"People who talk a lot about themselves seldom want to hear what others say."*

Of course, there are many things that we should not listen to, such as gossip (2 Timothy 2:14), but that is not the topic here.

I have found numerous quotes about listening from a book of quotes. Here are a few of my favorites:

- *"We have two ears to listen and one mouth to speak so that we can listen twice as much as we speak"* (Epictetus).[4]
- *"The world is dying for want, not of good preaching, but of good hearing"* (George Dana Boardman).[5]
- *"The first duty of love is to listen"* (Paul Tillich).[6]
- *"He who no longer listens to his brother will soon no longer be listening to God"* (Dietrich Bonhoeffer).[7]

Listening is a discipline! It takes patience, concentration and especially genuine concern for others to be a good listener. In a recent blog, motivational speaker John Maxwell said, *"Connecting with people is a two-way street. It is a dialogue, not a monologue."*8 It is something we should never forget as we take the time to listen to others.

I believe one of the world's greatest listeners was Job. Most of what was said to him was of little value, but they were his (so-called) friends, so out of either courtesy or other reasons, he listened. A leader at times has to listen to "Job's comforters." Over and over again in the book of Job, it says, *"Job replied."* He replied because he first *listened.*

A leader will never lack for appreciation if he or she is a good listener. Personally, I have gotten many a good sermon or teaching illustration from carefully listening. The most important person we need to listen to, of course, is God. Sometimes He speaks through others, even the least among us.

The following quote from H. Norman Wright in his book *Helping Those Who Hurt* sums up this chapter:

> *What do we mean by listening? What do we mean by hearing? Is there a difference? Definitely! Hearing involves gaining content or information for your own purposes. This isn't helping. Listening involves caring for and being empathetic toward the friend who is talking. Hearing means that you are concerned about what's going on inside you during the conversation. We've all done this. Listening means that you're trying to understand the feelings of the other person, and are*

listening for his or her sake. This is helping.[9]

21
CHEAP EDUCATION

Does not wisdom call out?
Does not understanding raise her voice?
(Proverbs 8:1, NIV)

In conjunction with the art of listening is the importance of who we listen to. My father taught me that it's possible to get the cheapest education just by listening: to grandparents, people with white hair (elderly), and even the least among us.

Wisdom does call out at times from the strangest places and people. I take notes, not only when listening to a sermon, but when listening to conversations in daily life. It always gives me joy when I hear my staff repeat something I have said, in either casual conversation or a staff meeting.

Occasionally, I will hear someone say something I have either never heard before or is contrary to my thinking. Or, it may be an insight that I have never thought about or taught. A light goes on in me, and I make a mental note to give further thought to what was said. I may end up adding this to my education. On several occasions, I have said to the person who just spoke: "You have just become my teacher. The teacher [me] has become a student in your classroom."

Out of the mouths of spiritual babes there can be incredible insights, wisdom and knowledge. Even a broken clock is right twice a day, such as when one of Job's so-called comforters said, *"It is not only the old who are wise, not only the aged who understand what is right"* (Job 32:9). I have to stop myself sometimes from rambling on and on, spilling out what I think is wisdom when it is not. Job told his ramblers, *"If only you would be altogether silent! For you, that would be wisdom"* (Job 13:5). A few verses later Job said, *"Listen carefully to my words; let your ears take in what I say."* Sometimes we need to just stop and listen to others.

Recently, at one of our banquets, one of our students was assigned to sit at a table of ten for fellowship. Later, I was told that one woman at the table dominated the entire evening with non-stop talk. "She even talked with food in her mouth," was the report. For those individuals, the evening was not very fulfilling. All leaders have encountered such people. May we not copy them!

Wisdom Shouts!

Wisdom really does shout in the streets in more ways than we may realize (See Proverbs 1:20). When we recognize wisdom from the streets, it's good to say within ourselves, *"I hear that! I receive that!"*

There is an old story of a young man who was out walking in the desert when a voice said to him, "Pick up some pebbles and put them in your pocket, and tomorrow you will be both sorry and glad." The young man obeyed. He stooped down and picked up a handful of pebbles and put them in his pocket. He decided one pocketful was enough. The next morning he reached into that pocket and found diamonds, rubies and emeralds! And he was both glad and sorry. Glad that he had taken some—sorry that he hadn't taken more!

So it is with education; whether it is formal or informal, from academics, theologians, parents, grand-parents, friends or neighbors. They may have some gem of an insight to share with us. This kind of education is much cheaper than the formal type. Sometimes common sense is common cents—worth many dollars!

"He who will never use the thoughts of other men's brains, proves that he has no brains"[1] (Charles Spurgeon).

"A person who graduates today and stops learning tomorrow is uneducated the day after."[2]

When I first arrived in New York City to join my brother David and to work with gangs and drug addicts, I was out of my element, to say the least! It was as if I had landed in a foreign land. The Holy Spirit showed me that I needed to have an interpreter by my side, someone who could translate the street and drug culture to me so that I could make the Gospel message relevant to the subculture. I chose a man my senior, a long-term drug addict that Christ had transformed, and I kept him by my side in ministering to other addicts and street people. I got a true education on the ways of the streets in the process. After some years, a convert from the drug culture said to me, "Pastor, you think like an addict." He meant it in a good way. His comment made me feel like I'd just been given a certificate of completion in my education in the "hood" as some inner-city neighborhoods are called.

I am going through one of life's new education courses as I write this. Now, in my senior years, I have returned to work with today's addicted population. However, this is a new century and those coming out of the drug culture reflect this era. They are not the gangs and drug abusers of the previous century. I am going through a learning curve getting re-educated.

I see too many pastors and leaders still speaking in the language of previous decades and generations. There are some wise men who have made observations about this:

- *"When a subject becomes totally obsolete, we make it a required course"* (Peter Drecker).[3]
- *"The secret of education is respecting the pupil"* (Ralph Waldo Emerson).[4]
- *"Pay attention and listen to the sayings of the wise"* (Proverbs 22:17, NIV). I might add, no matter who and where it comes from, if it lines up with the Word of God.

There are walking textbooks among us on a variety of subjects. It is a wise man or woman who keeps watch for them and listens as they speak. Sometimes educational wisdom is communicated in harsh words and can be rejected because of either its tone or the person who is dispensing the wisdom. How often do young people and adult children ignore their parent's instructions to their peril? *"It is better to heed a wise man's rebuke than to listen to the song of fools"* (Ecclesiastes 7:5, NIV). This lack of knowledge turned right side up, becomes an opportunity to learn. This is what I like to call, "cheap education." We can be thankful we don't know everything.

The kind of education I have been writing about should not be a substitute for formal and traditional education. My library is full of the wisdom from learned men and women. I agree with William James who said, *"To neglect the wise sayings of great thinkers is to deny ourselves our truest education."*[5]

However, the point of finding "cheap education" is that the classroom of life is full of valuable lessons to learn. Mark Twain said, *"I never let my schooling interfere with my education."*[6] Apparently, Mr. Twain had met many an educated fool!

Those who value a "cheap education" find knowledge, wisdom and education in the most unlikely places. Best-selling author Robert Fulghum wrote that, *"All I really need to know...I learned in kindergarten."*[7] He must have read Psalms 8:2: *"Out of the mouth of babes and sucklings hast thou ordained strength."*

I would be remiss if I did not support the idea of having a living mentor; preferably following a mentoring program, when offered. In the ministry of Teen Challenge, we call our residential program a discipleship/rehabilitation program. One of the most important parts is having more mature brothers and sisters mentoring the younger converts. Also, our staff is required to participate in mentoring classes. Two books I recommend are, *Spiritual Mentoring*[8] and *The Making of a Mentor.*[9]

Although I have never been a designated mentor to leaders who serve under me, I have conducted my ministry in such a way so as to be a mentoring example to others. Those close to me know I often talk about "teaching moments." However, there are many young ministers and Christian workers who do not have an official or unofficial mentor. In such cases, my recommendation is to seek out both living, as well as, dead mentors.

22
MOST OF MY MENTORS ARE DEAD

*Join with others following my example,
brothers, and take note of those who live
according to the pattern we gave you*
(Philippians 3:17).

We all need mentors, dead or alive. Most of mine are dead. As a teenager, I knew I was called to preach, so I asked my pastor father how to construct a sermon. He gave me a book of sermons by Clovis Chappel, and I studied those sermons carefully. Ever since, I have followed the style and format of how he constructed sermon notes. I also studied my father's sermon notes, as they were similar to Chappel's.

At the top of my list of mentors are my father and mother. Dad taught me the importance of studying the Word and how to treat people as important, no matter their rank in society. Both my parents, especially my mother, taught me the importance of prayer. My mother also taught me about giving. My brother David mentored me in more ways than he ever knew. Most mentors don't know who they are mentoring. It's a choice others make to follow, and not just the mentors themselves.

The majority of my other mentors are dead men and women, many whose biographies and books I have read. John Piper writes in his book, *Brothers, We are Not Professionals* of the importance of reading biographies. Here's an extensive quote from a chapter of that book entitled, *Brothers, Read Christian Biographies.*

Hebrews 11 is a divine mandate to read Christian biographies. The unmistakable implication of the chapter is that if we hear about the faith of our forefathers (and mothers), we will "...lay aside every weight, and sin" and "...run with endurance the race set before us" (Hebrews 12:1). If we asked the author [of Hebrews], "How shall we stir one another up to love and good works?" (10:24), his answer would be: "Through encouragement from the living (10:25) and the dead" (11:1-40). Christian biography is the means by which the body life of the church cuts across centuries.[1]

Piper continues:

The fellowship of the living and the dead is especially crucial for pastors. As leaders in the church, we are supposed to have vision for the future. We are supposed to declare prophetically where our church should be going. Not that God can't give vision and direction and inspiration. He regularly uses human agents to stir his people. So the question for us as pastors is: Through what agents does God give us vision and direction and inspiration? For me, one of the most important answers has been men and women of faith who, though dead, are yet speaking (Hebrews 11:4). Christian biography, well chosen, combines all sorts of things pastors need, but have little time to pursue.

The Reward of Great Men and Women

"The reward of great men is that, after they have died, one is not quite sure they are dead" (Jules Renard).[2]

Here is a list of some of my mentors that have gone on to heaven:

1. C. T. Studd (1860-1931), a famous English cricket player who gave away his wealth and went as a missionary to China, and then to India. A quote of his I have adopted for my life is, *"Some want to live within sound of a church and chapel bell. I want to run a rescue ship within a yard of Hell!"*[3]

2. J. Hudson Taylor (1832-1905) the founder of the China Inland Mission was noted for not accepting funds at meetings in which he spoke in his homeland of England. I learned from him the importance of praying for workers for the harvest field. One of my favorite quotes of his is, *"I have found there are three stages to every work of God; first, it is impossible, then, it is difficult, then, it is done."*[4]

3. Charles H. Spurgeon (1834-92) was England's best-known preacher of the second half of the 19th century who became pastor of London's famed New Park Street Church at the age of 20. In 1861 the church moved to the Metropolitan Tabernacle where Spurgeon's congregation numbered more than 10,000 people. His printed sermons are voluminous, including his most famous, *The Treasury of David*. Choosing from Spurgeon's quotes is difficult as they are some of the best I have read. Here is a sampling: *"The true minister of Christ knows that the true value of a sermon must lie, not in its fashion and manner, but in the truth which it conveys. The grandest discourse*

ever delivered is an ostentatious failure if the doctrine of God's grace is absent from it."[5]

Some of my other mentors are: C. S. Lewis, A. W. Tozer, F. B. Meyer, and Oswald Chambers. From Martin Luther, I have learned both from his poor as well his positive examples—in addition to enjoying some of his writings. There are numerous biographies I have read and enjoyed, the latest being on the life of Dietrich Bonheoffer by Eric Metaxas entitled *Dietrich Bonhoeffer Pastor, Martyr, Prophet, Spy.*

Of course, the Bible is full of heroes of the faith, but so is history. Some others in my personal Hall of Fame are Billy Graham, George Mueller, Fannie Crosby, D. L. Moody, Susanna Wesley, her sons Charles and John Wesley, Charles Finney, George Whitefield, Eric Liddell *(Chariots of Fire),* and Martin Luther King, Jr.

A man called Charles "Tremendous" Jones (no one ever gave me such a tremendous nickname) said, *"You are the same today that you are going to be in five years from now except for two things: the people with whom you associate and the books you read."*[6] At the time of this writing, I am reading *George Washington's Sacred Fire* by Peter Lillback about the faith, Christian beliefs and practices of our first president.[7]

When I go into a pastor's study, I immediately look at his bookshelves. If he should step out of his office, I look more closely at the book titles, for I can tell a lot about him by the books he reads. My wife told me once that I had so many books that I might have to choose between her and my books. I said, "Honey, I'll miss you." (Just kidding!) Yes, even the Bible reminds us, *"Of the making of books there is no end"* (Ecclesiastics 12:12).

In the end, I agree with A. W. Tozer who wrote: *"To think without the proper amount of good reading is to limit our thinking to our own tiny crop of ground. The crop cannot be large...To observe only and neglect reading is to deny ourselves the immense value of other people's observations, and since the better books are written by trained observers, the loss is sure to be enormous."*[8]

I often ask young ministers which Bible character they would most want to be like, after Jesus. Our most important mentors are in the Scriptures, and although all of them are important, it is good to identify those whom you might want to emulate. My favorites are Caleb in the Old Testament and Barnabas (the Encourager) in the New Testament. Jesus said, *"I have set you an example that you should do as I have done"* (John 13:15). The purpose of following and learning from anyone's life (living or dead), is to discover the Jesus in them and do as He did through their lives. The Apostle Paul writes, *"Join with others in following my example, brothers, and take note of those who live according to the pattern we gave you"* (Philippians 3:17).

Of course, we need living mentors at all stages of our lives. It's my experience that many leaders do not want the obligation of being an official mentor (coach is often the word used now for mentoring). However, there is nothing stopping us from selecting someone and watching how they conduct their lives for the lessons we can learn. *"It is more important to watch how a man lives, than to listen to what he says"* (Croft Pentz).[9] One godly example is worth a thousand persuasions or arguments!

23

BEWARE OF THE PRESUMPTION
OF FRIENDSHIPS

If someone asks Him, "What are these wounds on your body?" He will answer, "The wounds I was given in the house of my friends" (Zechariah 13:6).

After the friendship of God, a friend's affection is the greatest treasure here below (Source unknown).

A very close friend of mine will often say to me when asking for a favor, "Please, let me know if you feel I'm taking advantage of our friendship." How I wish others would say and do the same. There can be a downside to friendship. It's when someone we call a friend may unintentionally violate normal standards of friendship.

I fear in writing this that a few of my friends may wonder if they have been presumptive in our friendship. The good thing about friends is that their mistakes are easy to forgive. So, I write this for myself, that I may be careful to not take advantage of the friendship and generosity of others, and so the reader might do the same. An ancient quote addresses this problem: *"The man who throws a stone at the birds scares them away, and the man who abuses a friend destroys friendship"* (Source unknown).

The mother of the two sons of Zebedee presumed on the relationship of Jesus. Their mother went to Jesus and asked a bold thing of Him. She said,

"Grant that these two sons of mine may sit at your right and the other at your left in your kingdom" (Matthew 20:20-21). Talk about presumption! Her sons probably asked their mother to intercede for their ambitions. Whichever the case, Jesus calmly answered that He wasn't the One that would be making that decision!

Consider What a Friend *is* and What a Friend *is not!*

A friend:
1. Is someone who goes around saying nice things about you behind your back!
2. *"Is a present you give yourself"* (Robert Louis Stevenson).[1]
3. Is someone who will attack you from the front!
4. Is a shock absorber for the bumps of life.
5. Is someone who knows all about you, and likes you just the same.
6. Does not rub it in when you make a fool of yourself.
7. Will challenge you to get closer to God.
8. Makes you feel good about yourself.
9. Is someone who comes in when the whole world goes out!
10. *"If one falls down, his friend will help him"* (Proverbs 4:10).
11. Will remember your birthday, but forget how many you have had!

Now, on the other hand...there are friends who are not friends in the truest sense of the word. Mark Twain said, *"The holy passion of friendship is of sweet and steady and loyal and enduring a nature that it will last through a whole lifetime, if not asked for money."*[2] Frances de Sales aptly stated in the 17th century a truism about friends: *"Friendship based on mutual material profit is not true friendship, since it is not based on true love."*[3] Proverbs 27:6 says, *"Faithful are the wounds of a friend."* A true friend wounds as a doctor who performs surgery to remove a cancer. A so-called friend wounds in ways that do not bring healing, but deep hurt instead.

A friend is not:

1. Someone who does you a favor and immediately expects a payback in return.

2. Someone who makes you feel uncomfortable in asking for a favor.

3. Someone who is a "user."

4. Someone who expects you to connect them with one of your other friends to ask that friend to do something for them based on your friendship with that person. Got it?

5. Someone who will break off a relationship with you when you show mercy to someone they disrespect, or with whom they have a broken relationship.

6. Someone who cuts off their friendship with you if it is going to cost them something; such as, if the friend has been dismissed from a church or organization and it is implied your friendship with that person should break off.

7. Someone who will reschedule appointments with you if a better offer comes along.

8. Someone who will flatter you to your face, but talk ill of you behind your back.

9. Someone who uses you as a stepping stone to get to someone they feel is more useful to them.

10. Someone who will ask how you are, and never mean it.

Good Friends Last a Lifetime

I'm sure we've all had other experiences with friends, both good and bad, not listed above. However, it's been my experience that good friends last a lifetime.

Charles Swindoll writes, *"Friends are those whose lives are like branches. They provide shade; they provide refuge from the demanding, irritating and searing rays of the hot sun. You can find comfort by them. You can find strength near them. They are tree-like in that they bear fruit that provides nourishment and encouragement."*[4]

A friend will not ask you to compromise your principles for the sake of friendship. Our relationship to friends should be based on Psalm 119:63: *"I am a friend to all who fear You, to all who follow Your precepts."* Ralph Waldo Emerson wrote, "God evidently does not intend us all to be rich, or powerful or great, but He does intend us all to be friends."[5]

The greatest compliment it seems to me that anyone can make regarding friendship is to be called a friend of our Lord. Moses was given the privilege of speaking face to face with the Lord *"...as a man speaketh to a friend"* (Exodus 33:11, KJV). One of my favorite New Testament verses is John 15:15. *"I no longer call you servants, because a servant does not know his master's business. Instead, I have called you friends, for everything that I learned from the Father, I have made known to you."*

Even when some of the disciples went back to their old business as fishermen after Jesus' resurrection, He did not give up on them. It appears they may have given up on Him. Jesus found the disciples fishing and called to them, *"Friends haven't you any fish?"* This is what friends do—stick with you no matter what.

> *Show me a man's closest companions and I will make a fairly accurate guess as to what sort of man he is, as well as what sort of man he is likely to become* (Howard and William Hendricks).[6]

> *To be rich in friends is to be poor in nothing* (Lilian Whiting).[7]

> *It's interesting! You sign a contract for marriage, a license to drive a car, a mortgage to own a home, a W-2 form for a job, an agreement to join a health club, but there are no documents to bind you to a friendship. No sealed stamp of commitment. No official guidelines, unless you consider God's Word!* (Traci Mullins)[8]

I know that at times I have disappointed people who sought a closer relationship with me (as a friend) and for certain reasons I was unable to do so. I am sensitive to this because I have been on the other side, seeking to be a friend to someone who did not respond. However, friendships must take place naturally (or in some cases supernaturally), or it is not true friendship.

Facebook "friends" are a new phenomenon of the Internet age and this would necessitate a whole chapter of its own to analyze! I prefer the old-fashioned way of building friendships. Someone has said a true friend will tell you when your face is dirty—very hard to do with Facebook "friends". However, I am growing to appreciate the fact that on a certain level, we can have friends at a distance and even unmet friends that Facebook enables. But it should never be a substitute for having face-to-face friends or voice-to-voice friends via the telephone.

Croft Pentz has written in his book, *1001 Things Your Mother Told You* that "...*a friend is someone who is there for you at the drop of a tear.*" We all need those kinds of friends beside us, and we need to cherish them as long as we live.[9]

24

THE SHRINKING PULPIT

I did not shrink from declaring to you the
whole purpose of God (Acts 20:27, NAS).

A lesson my father taught me was to preach *"the whole counsel of God."* This he based on the Apostle Paul's farewell message to the church at Ephesus, recorded in Acts 20:16-38. His last words to them are a challenge to all who Paul called *"overseers that shepherd the church of God."*

Acts 20:20 and verse 27 are translated in the NAS, *"I did not shrink from declaring to you everything that was profitable, and teaching you from house to house...for I did not shrink from declaring to you the whole purpose of God."*

The King James Version translated *"the whole purpose of God"* as *"the whole counsel of God."* Over and over my father emphasized this important call in his pastoral role—that it was his duty to preach the *whole counsel of God.* I knew this meant to cover all the necessary doctrines in the Scriptures, so as to produce full-grown, mature disciples of Christ.

Unfortunately, today we see the shrinking of the pulpit. The whole counsel of God and the full-gospel have been replaced with a half counsel and half Gospel. Certain teachings on sacrifice, suffering, God's wrath and judgment, or what's considered "negative" messages, are missing from some pulpits.

When I was privileged to be one of the founding pastors of Times Square Church, people would approach me after a message and comment that they had never heard such preaching. I knew it was not because I was some outstanding preacher. I was simply preaching the whole counsel of God, the kind of messages I had grown up under. I discovered that many who visited our church had come from a one-message church. In some cases, all the believer ever heard was the faith and prosperity message, or preaching on holiness, or only salvation sermons, or only end-time prophecy messages.

Spiritual Vitamin B Deficiency

I discovered those coming from some churches suffered from spiritual vitamin B deficiency. The B stands for Bible and some pulpits were neglecting certain biblical truths in their teaching and preaching. One message I preached was entitled, *"Why Sit We Here Till We Die,"* based on Second Kings 7:3. That message brought in a whole group of new regular attendees.

Charles Swindoll tells the story of a preacher giving a lecture on the Minor Prophets, one after another. He finally came to the book of Amos. "We have now come to Amos," he said, "and what shall we do with Amos?" A man sitting in the rear of the church said, loud enough to be heard by everyone, "He can have my seat! I'm going home!"[1] Some people just aren't open to hearing the truth and power that comes from God's Word.

A lot of seats are empty in churches because of a shrinking pulpit. Some pastors fear losing people if they don't preach a user-friendly, soft message; yet the opposite can be just as true. Many people are hungry for the whole counsel of God because they eventually realize the meals they are being served have little meat, and a whole lot of milk (See Hebrews 5:12).

W. A. Criswell (1909-2002) was the pastor of the famous First Baptist Church in Dallas, Texas. When he became the pastor there, he told the deacons he was going to preach week by week through the Bible. He was asked, "What are we going to do when you preach from Leviticus and the Minor Prophets? We're going to lose people."

"I promise you, we will not lose, but instead, gain people," Criswell replied. Sure enough, after that, people in the church would ask one another, "What book did you get saved in?" Some got saved when Criswell preached from the Minor Prophets, and some even when hearing sermons from Leviticus.

History tells us that Thomas Jefferson physically cut out of his New Testament all references to Jesus' miracles and His divinity. Some preachers I hear today ought to have their Bible called the Thin Bible, as they only preach from selected texts.

The term "full gospel" when I was growing up in the church meant we believed in and taught the necessity of the baptism of the Holy Spirit. We do need that baptism, but we also need a "full gospel" that does not neglect *any* of the truths Jesus taught. I once preached a message entitled, *"Wows, Woos and Woes."* The Word will "wow" us with its promises, "woo" [meaning seek] us by the Holy Spirit, and send "woes" when we persist in walking in disobedience (See Jeremiah 17:16, KJV). John 16:13 tells us that when the Holy Spirit comes, He will be *"the Spirit of truth"* and *"will guide you into all truth."*

The Day of the Specialist

John Piper writes in *Brothers We Are Not Professionals* about tolerance as it affects today's preaching and preachers. He says, *"Beware of replacing real, truth-based tolerance with spurious professional tolerance...for every pastor who enjoys respect in spite of prophetic faithfulness to the cross, a hundred pastors enjoy that respect because the cross has been compromised."*[2] My prayer is not to be numbered among the latter.

In many ways, pastors have become like physicians. It used to be that doctors were general practitioners, able to treat most kinds of sicknesses. Today is the day of the "specialist" in the medical field. One only has to look up physicians in the Yellow Pages (used before search engines) to see that this is true. Some pastors are biblical specialists: one emphasizes faith, another prophecy, and others prosperity, deliverance, inner healing, seeker-friendliness or positive thinking. But it is more important for pastors to preach the whole counsel of God. Vance Havner said, *"It is not the business of the preacher to fill the house. It is his business to fill the pulpit."*[3]

I don't know of any more powerful statements on the importance of the pulpit and the preacher than Charles Haddon Spurgeon, who began pastoring the London Metropolitan Tabernacle when he was twenty-seven years old, often preaching to crowds of up to 6,000 people. His statements on preaching and the preacher are as powerful today as when he first spoke them. For example, he said the preacher must never feel it is easy to preach, but to put everything he had into it; and that before he came to the pulpit he trembled like an aspen leaf.

Regarding preaching, Spurgeon stated, *"Sometimes after preaching the Gospel, I have been so filled with self-reproach that I could hardly sleep through the night, because I had not preached as I desired. I have sat down and cried over some sermons, as though I knew I had missed the mark and lost the opportunity. Not once or twice, but many a time it has happened that within a few days someone has come to tell me that he found the Lord through that very sermon, the shortcoming of which I deplored. Glory to Jesus, it was His gentleness that did it."*[4]

The seeker-friendly message of today has created a church that Chuck Colson has called, *"a mile wide and an inch deep."*[5] Some people long for the "good ole days," and I am one of them when it comes to what comes forth from the pulpit.

When I went to Bible College, I noted after getting to know many fellow students that some came to school more mature in the Word and in character than others. Being curious, I began asking questions and made an important discovery. Those who sat under strong preachers/teachers were much further in their spiritual development than those who did not have such a privilege. I also discovered that those advanced students were usually from churches where the pastor had served a long tenure.

Another Spurgeon quote is in order. *"Avoid a sugared Gospel as you would shun sugar of lead (a 19th century sweet-tasting poison). Seek that Gospel which rips up and tears and cuts and wounds and hacks and even kills, for that is the Gospel that makes alive again. And when you have found it, give good heed to it. Let it enter into your inmost being. As the rain soaks into the ground, so pray that the Gospel soaks into your soul."*[6] I might add, pray that it soaks into the pastors, preachers and evangelists who are given the task of occupying the pulpit—any pulpit.

25
HOW TO PLAY SECOND FIDDLE

"He must increase, but I must decrease"
(John 3:30).

Leonard Bernstein was asked to name the most difficult instrument to play. He responded, *"Second fiddle."* To all the "assistants" who read this: assistant pastors, assistant directors, assistant managers and whoever is second in command or below, I dedicate this brief chapter. I know how to play "second fiddle". I've done it well, and I've done it not so well.

In case you don't know what a second fiddle is, here's a few names: Aaron, Joshua, Elisha, John the Baptist and his disciples, Peter, Barnabas and Titus to name just a few Bible characters. These all served under a better-known pastor or leader. Others in modern times are Franklin Graham or Andy Stanley and those who serve behind the scenes. My parents named me Donald, but I use the short form of Don. In some cultures, a "Don" is known as a leader. I was speaking in a country in the southern hemisphere, and was asked to invite the local drug lord to come hear me speak. I met him in a marketplace and was introduced to a man simply referred to as "The Don." We may have both been "Dons," but we lived worlds apart, in every way. Thankfully, he did come to hear me share the Gospel that night, sitting right up in front.

Of course, my parents did not want me to be that kind of a "Don," for they gave me the middle name of Wesley after John and Charles Wesley, the founders of the Methodist movement. With that name,

I am certain my parents hoped that I would enter the ministry. A few years earlier, my parents named my brother David, and we all know that David in the Bible became a king. A king is *higher* in rank than a don, and I've had to live with that all my life. The point is that I have known how to live in the shadow of a well-known and respected leader, pastor, and author who happened to be my brother. I worked under David for years, first in a para-church organization and later in the pioneering of a famous church.

Always Second in Command

From this experience as second in command, I have learned some very important lessons:

1. No matter whom you may serve under, always know who *you* are and what your *spiritual gifts* are in relationship to the person you serve.

My brother made it very easy to serve under him, for he always recognized, appreciated and acknowledged my spiritual gifts. Many who serve a man or woman of God do not get the recognition that I did. I listed Titus above as being a "second fiddle". I don't know that he was, as evidenced from Paul's letter to him, but I know from sermons I have preached and heard, that Titus seems to always get second billing to Timothy. It surprised me a few years ago to discover that Titus' name is mentioned 13 times in the New Testament and Timothy's only 7 times. When names are mentioned in association with Paul's missionary journeys, the two names that come to my mind are Barnabas and Timothy, not Titus; yet his name is as closely linked to Paul's name as anyone else. Titus is on my "second fiddle" list because Paul left him in Crete alone to help set the church there in order. It was a very out of the way place (Titus 1:3).

Whoever and wherever we serve, first, we need to focus on the Lord who calls us. Second, we need to know that He is the One who has placed us under or beside the leader, and that we serve God together. Martin Luther said, *"A Christian is the most free lord of all, and subject to none; a Christian is the most dutiful servant of all, and subject to all."*[1]

2. Get used to people approaching you and asking you how so-and-so is (in my case it was my brother), and never asking how you are.

Joe DiMaggio was one of the greatest baseball hitters of all time, but he had two brothers who also played in the major leagues. Did you know that? I can just imagine how often they were asked about their more famous brother!

John the Baptist's disciples found it difficult to be suddenly overshadowed by some new disciples following another leader. *"Jesus was gaining and baptizing more disciples than John"* (John 4:1). They were being confronted by the Pharisees who asked them about the differences between John's disciples and Jesus' disciples. John the Baptist's response is a good principle to follow for anyone serving another: *"He must increase, but I must decrease"* (John 3:30).

If you have a famous father, sibling, uncle or grandparent, my advice to you is every time someone asks you about that well-known person, take it as a compliment, and not a personal slight. You can choose your friends, but you can't choose your family or relatives—for better or worse. The sooner you come to terms with the idea that it is better to have someone famous in your family than someone infamous, the better your own life will be! The same advice goes for those who serve under a highly visible leader. Believe me, many envy you for being given such an honor to serve where you serve and who you serve under.

3. Get used to people using you to get to the person you serve.

I recall a Bible college buddy calling me to ask if I could get my brother David to speak at his church on a Sunday night. We were in his city at the time conducting a large evangelism crusade. My friend said, "Your brother could help me build my church almost overnight if he spoke here." I told him I was sorry, but with our schedule, I couldn't grant his request. He never spoke to me again.

Sometimes it is the function of an assistant to screen requests for the person they serve, and the leader may leave it to the judgment of that assistant as to whether the appointment is made. It takes wisdom to discern whether such an opening should be given for the person to meet with the leader.

The sons of Zebedee's mother went to Jesus, probably sent by James and John, to ask Jesus for a high-ranking position in His kingdom when He overturned the Roman rule of their land (See Matthew 20:20-17). This was a case of Jesus' disciples thinking a mother had more pull than they did.

4. Guard your heart from jealousy.

One of the healthiest spiritual and emotional things that can help us serve on any level in the church and ministry is to be secure in your calling and giftings. You may have a leadership gift, but need time to learn from the leader/pastor you serve. You may be destined to become *the* lead pastor or head of a ministry, but be too young yet for such a position. Or, you may be called to a lifetime of serving under others.

Exodus chapter 12 relates the story of Miriam, Moses' sister, and Aaron challenging his leadership. *"'Has the Lord only spoken through Moses?' they asked. Hasn't he also spoken through us?'"* (vs. 1-2) Miriam's name is mentioned first, before Aaron, in regards to the questioning of Moses. I assume from this that she was the instigator. She apparently was jealous of Moses' wife. *"And the Lord heard it!"* The Lord affirmed Moses' leadership (12:5-8), and temporarily inflicted Miriam with leprosy, putting her out of the congregation for seven days (12:15).

In Galatians 5:20, jealousy is listed in bad company along with idolatry, witchcraft, hatred, discord, fits of rage, selfish ambition, dissentions, factions, envy and drunkenness. That's a gang of bad guys to stay away from.

"There is not a single soul that jealousy looks good on. Nobody! It looks ugly on everybody, and it makes us act ugly—it makes us act out of character" (Beth Moore).[2]

5. Don't see your position and place as more important than it is!

I have seen too many assistants think they are in charge, rather than the one they serve. Certain assistants are given a great deal of authority and any amount of authority can be misused or abused. Some assistants can be overly protective of the one they serve.

On the other hand, we often read in the newspaper or hear in the media of some assistant who stole money, ideas, or other things, taking advantage of their position next to the one with fame or power. When Christian assistants begin speaking in the name of the person they serve without the knowledge and authority of that person, this misuse of authority usually ends up hurting the church and the leader. Even though Paul was a strong leader, he called himself the least of the apostles (See 1 Corinthians 15:9).

Henrietta Mears said, *"The man who keeps busy helping the man below him won't have time to envy the man above him."*[3]

6. Always remember, "Promotion comes from above" (and I don't mean a higher earthly power).

Psalm 75:6 says that exultation, or promotion, comes neither from the east or the west nor the south. The inference is therefore that it comes from the north, meaning heaven above. The next verse confirms this: *"But God is the Judge: He puts down one and exalts another."*

My testimony is that I actually ran away from leadership more than I desired it. Leadership was thrust upon me, and I came to accept it over time. Having grown up in a pastor's home, I saw early on the negative or difficult side of being the one in charge, such as responsibility, rejection, and financial challenges. I was more like Gideon than the sons of Zebedee!

I have seen ambition ruin some leaders. Most men and women in the Bible who were mightily used of God were either reluctant leaders or were so seized by God that they knew they must obey His calling to serve: Moses, Samuel, Saul in his youth (who hid when Samuel wanted to anoint him), Esther, Isaiah, Jonah, etc.

A pastor friend of mine once told me he felt that he was called to be a "second fiddle." Then he added, "Since I've accepted this, God has allowed me to play in some of the greatest spiritual orchestras in the world."

26
THE ECONOMICS OF SALVATION

For this is what the Lord says:
"You were sold for nothing, and without
money you will be redeemed" (Isaiah 52:3).

I watched our Teen Challenge choir singing on one occasion and decided to do a quick calculation. There were 24 members of the choir. Based on past knowledge of drug addicts and alcoholics, I estimated the total number of years the 24 had spent on drugs and came up with the figure of 250 years.

Next, I estimated the years they had spent in prison, and came up with an unscientific number of 75. Then I wondered how much money taxpayers had spent to pay for their prison time and hospital visits to get detoxified. I came up with a very conservative figure of 1.8 million dollars.

After the choir sang, I went forward to share a message on the ministry of Teen Challenge, and in the course of my message, I mentioned the above figures. Then I said, "Jesus saves" and let the words sink in for a moment. Finally, the audience got the point and clapped. I had just arrived at a very important aspect of salvation that we rarely think about; that is, the *Economics of Salvation*.

I continued, "As you heard those 24 members of the choir praising the Lord, I want you to realize that the government and the taxpayers are no longer spending money for their incarceration or their medical treatment from the adverse effects of drugs and alcohol. And innocent people are no longer losing money and goods to these individuals who once robbed to support their addiction."

Then I smiled and said, "I think I'm going to send the government a bill for Jesus' services. *Jesus saves* is not just a theological statement—it's an economic statement, as well. Salvation is free, but its effects create the saving of lives and the saving of money.

Smoking, drinking and gambling can put a deep hole in a monthly budget. Sin is expensive. (I realize that non-smokers and non-drinkers can waste money on other "acceptable" pleasures that a Christian might spend their money on, such as entertainment and food. This is not good stewardship, either.) But generally speaking, a true biblical Christian enjoys an economic blessing when not supporting a smoking, drug or alcohol habit.

Wisdom of the Ages

"In the house of the wise are stores of choice food and oil, but a foolish man devours all he has. He who pursues righteousness and love finds life, prosperity and honor" (Proverbs 21:20-21). I have witnessed the spiritual, physical and financial loss that comes from addictive habits. The costs to society and the taxpayer from the adverse effects of smoking alone are enormous. Add to that the hidden costs of absenteeism at work, as well as accidents, theft, and medical costs of those that abuse drugs and/or alcohol in the workplace. The taxes added to tobacco and alcohol are often called "sin tax." In no way do they cover the true costs of the adverse effects on such so-called pleasures.

Proverbs 21:17 says, *"He who loves pleasure will become poor; whoever loves wine and oil will never be rich.*" Proverbs 23:19-21 has a similar warning: *"Listen, my son, and be wise, and keep your heart on the right path. Do not join those who drink too much wine or gorge themselves on meat, for drunkards and gluttons become poor, and drowsiness clothes them in rags."*

Our national debt soars higher and higher, like an out-of-control heroin or cocaine addict. I wonder what a national, spiritual awakening might do to save our spiraling health care costs and other costs generated from a lifestyle of sin. One person who quits smoking can save approximately 60 dollars a month from the price of cigarettes alone, and more money if they stop drinking alcohol. Other medical and health related savings may be difficult to estimate, but the reality is that Jesus can and does "save" us in more ways than one.

On a personal level, believers save money if they abstain from the world's vices. This is a principle taught throughout the Scriptures. Consider what might be a lifetime of savings if the smoker or drinker puts that same amount of money in a savings account, perhaps to leave an inheritance to their grandchildren (See Proverbs 13:22).

> *"The blessing of the Lord brings wealth, and he adds no trouble to it"* (Proverbs 10:22).

> *"He who pursues righteousness and love finds life, prosperity and honor"* (Proverbs 21:21).

> *"The house of the righteous contains great treasure, but the income of the wicked brings them trouble"* (Proverbs 15:6). (One trouble that often comes is bad health.)

A godly lifestyle is an investment for eternity, as well as good financial budgeting. Jesus saves souls and saves lives, and He can help us save money in ways you may have never considered. Of all the teachings and sermons I have ever heard that have to do with the improper use of money, few point out that a godly lifestyle is rewarded in financial savings, as well as soul saving.

Proverbs 13:22 is a promise that is fulfilled in the economics of salvation: *"Good people leave an inheritance to their grandchildren, but the sinner's wealth passes to the godly."*

27

THE TRANS-GENERATIONAL CHURCH

*I will teach you hidden lessons from the
past☐ ☐ stories we have heard and known,
stories our ancestors handed down to us.
We will not hide these truths from our
children but tell the next generation*
(Psalm 78:2-4).

One of the greatest needs in the church today is
to change the culture and programming so that there
are relationships and fellowship between the older and
younger generations. Even many youth leaders and
young pastors are seeing that it is not spiritually
and emotionally healthy to always exclude youth and
young adults from older adults and seniors. I have
seen too many youth groups, for example, operate
almost as a para-church group within the church. In
today's culture this is not good.

The latest U.S. Census reveals that non-married
couples represent 48 percent of households, leaving
many children and teens without a father figure in
the home—although, in some cases, there may be a
male in the house who is not the father. This does not
provide much security for children, as the male can
up and leave any time.

A pastor friend of a large urban church told me
that the majority of children and youth in his church
have no father, and in too many cases a grandparent
is raising the youngsters. An old Chinese proverb says,
"In a broken nest are few whole eggs."[1] In my work
in Teen Challenge, it is the exception when we see both

a mother and father involved in the lives of their children.

Does the church have a responsibility to make up for this loss? Yes and no! Only a full-time, godly husband or male can make up for the loss of a biological father. However, young people need more role models in their lives, and the church can help supply this.

I picked out a book from my personal library on how churches can change and grow, and there was not one paragraph on the importance of reaching youth. I have observed over the years that Billy Graham always gave attention in his preaching, in his crusade evangelism, and his writings to youth. Graham wrote this about young people: *"Millions of young people are shifting from one side to the other. They are like unguided missiles filled with energy and ambition and yet, somehow not 'fitting in'. Peer pressure leads them astray..."*[2] The church can help young people fight peer pressure by adult spiritual mentors and role models.

How can this be done? What can the church do to promote trans-generational relationships?

1. Provide opportunities for all ages to worship together.

This can be a daunting challenge, as each generation has its own musical tastes. This issue needs to be addressed by challenging each group to appreciate and sing the others Christian music preferences. The young people will be harder to convince, perhaps, than their elders to sing, on occasion, the others music. To quote a verse of the Bible and contextualize it to this subject: *"Be kindly affectioned one to another with brotherly love; in honor preferring one another,"* including having an appreciation for each other's worship music (Romans 12:10, NKJV).

One church has 45 minutes of worship each Sunday with all ages worshiping together, but also has learning and group activities together. *"We're challenging adults to understand that God entrusted them with a deposit of faith that is meant to be shared, not just with their children, but with an entire generation."* (Pastor Keith Spenser of Trinity Lutheran Church; Pembroke Pines, Florida.)

2. Plan family-wide events that include as many generations as possible.

Many of the young people in Teen Challenge have never seen families that can be holy and spiritually whole, and yet laugh and have fun. The church should plan events that include everyone: unified families, broken families, blended families, married couples, single parents, widows and widowers, senior couples and others.

Not only should the entire church worship together, but they should have times of fellowship together. Each year at Brooklyn Teen Challenge, we take our staff and students and spend a week camping together. Many of them have not known such fun times. It is a financial challenge for us to do so, but the effect on the students (from teens to older students) is profound.

3. Do a biblical teaching on the responsibility of one generation to another.

Here are a few verses to teach from:

• *"From the lips of children and infants you have ordained praise"* (Psalm 8:2). This shows the importance of children. For the older generation to not always be living in the past, they need to mix with the younger generation and know their likes, interests and challenges. It's not as important how old you are, but how you are, regardless of your age. *"The error of youth is to believe that intelligence is a substitute for experience, while the error of age is to believe experience is a substitute for intelligence"* (Lyman Bryson).[3]

• *"Come my children and listen to me; I will teach you the fear of the Lord"* (Psalm 34:11). The home is the best teaching place for children. I have seen wonderful products of a single parent home; but the church certainly can help such a parent bear this burden. The importance of knowing the faithfulness of the Lord over a lifetime is one reason older adults need to share with young people. This is revealed in the following Scripture:

• *"I was young and now I am old, yet I have never seen the righteous forsaken or their children begging bread. They are always generous and lend freely; their children will be blessed"* (Psalm 37:25-26, NIV).

> *Youth culture needs wise caretakers, good teachers to help youth learn to read the deeper meanings of experience, and help them understand and appreciate the real rewards of life* (Jeff Leeland).[4]

• *"We will not hide these truths from our children but tell the next generation about the glorious deeds of the Lord. We will tell of his power and the mighty miracles he has done"* (Psalm 78:4). Psalm 78 goes on to say that if the Israelites did not teach the younger generation how God's power gave them victory over their enemies, the newer generation would not have the courage to engage in warfare. They had weapons (bows), but were afraid to use them (v. 9). The church today can have a new generation that lacks faith and courage to challenge the issues of this era if they do not hear (and listen to) the testimonies of God's faithfulness to their elders.

• *"For even if you have ten thousand others to teach you about Christ, you have only one spiritual father. For I became your father in Christ Jesus when I preached the gospel to you"* (1 Corinthians 4:15). In a day when so many families are broken up and or dysfunctional, the church must do more than preach the Good News. We need to show it, especially to the youth. Whether the church wants to or not, it needs to provide spiritual fathers and mothers for young men and women. If it does not, the drop-out rate of young people in the church will only increase.

"When we are out of sympathy with the youth, then I think our work in this world is over."[5] This was said by an older man named George Macdonald. I might add, when the youth are out of sympathy for the older generation, their world will be too small. We need to build trans-generational churches and ministries. Amen?

28
CALLED TO THE OTHER SIDE

That day when evening came, he said to his disciples,
"Let us go over to the other side" (Mark 4:35).

They thought they knew where they were going. They voiced no concern or complaint when Jesus said, *"Let us go over to the other side."* There was no reluctance in getting into the boat with Jesus. Had they not witnessed the power of God as it flowed through Him to heal withered hands and all other order of malady? Had they not heard the screams of unclean spirits being evicted from those they tormented as they fell down before Him? His teaching in the local synagogue left them in awe many times. After all they had seen and heard, why would they ever be reluctant to go to the other side with Jesus?

And now, as He stood on a Galilean hillside, Jesus handpicked each of them by calling out their names: Simon, James, John (the brother of James), Andrew, Philip, Bartholomew, Matthew, Thomas, James, Thaddeus, Simon the Zealot, and Judas Iscariot (Mark 3:16-19). They were called, authorized, and sent out. Great! But why were they called? For what were they given authority? To whom were they being sent? They were about to find out.

These, whom Jesus called, authorized and sent out, came from a variety of backgrounds, having a variety of different talents and abilities. Some were tax collectors, while others were fishermen. Some had extreme political views, while others wanted only to make a quiet living. Ultimately, they would all answer the call that Jesus issued to them to serve the Lord in many different ways. They were a cross section of average people just like us. And though we are all very different, we all have the same destination: *the other side.*

Finding the Other Side

What or where is *the other side? The other side* is the place where we are called to minister the grace of God to bound and hurting people. *The other side* is where the character of Christ that has been formed in us now begins to flow from us. We arrive to minister on *the other side* by faith in the heart of God alone. Our journey will sometimes be greeted by the waves of conflict or confusion that threaten to swamp and destroy us. Our ministry on *the other side* may not be what we expected. It may be much better.

The Gospel account of Jesus' crossing over to *the other side* is only a few verses long. The disciples got into a boat with Jesus to cross over to *the other side.* In the midst of their mission, they encountered the wind and waves of a terrible storm, which Jesus silenced with a word. Once the storm was over, Jesus and the disciples reached *the other side,* arriving in the region called Decapolis, which means Ten Cities. Geographically, the Decapolis was located on the southeastern side of the Sea of Galilee. This place of Ten Cities was a place of Greek culture that emphasized pleasure over godliness, and reason over righteousness. It was a place of violence and wealth that glorified sexuality and human idolatry. They were the "sin cities" of their time, like our present-day San Francisco, New Orleans, and New York City.

Greek or Hellenistic culture, philosophy, and mythology had made inroads into generations of young Jewish minds. The Pharisees, who were devoted to keeping God's people faithful to the Torah, constantly admonished young Jews to separate themselves from this influence. This worldly influence crowded in around the Jewish people, affecting even the language that they spoke hundreds of years before Greek had become the language of commerce among all the nations in the Middle East. Gradually, the purity of the Jewish culture, which was centered on the God of Israel, was being displaced by this worldly and humanistic influence.

When Jesus invited the disciples to go to *the other side,* the very words carried a meaning that the disciples readily understood. They were going to a place where no devout religious Jew would have ventured. When they stepped off the boat in the Decapolis, they became the first "foreign missionaries." They had gone beyond their culture, beyond their experience, beyond their own religious traditions. It was a place where they would all be stretched and challenged by the things they saw and heard. They were going to the place that all disciples are called to, authorized, and sent.

Jesus was demonstrating to disciples of all ages that He was unwilling to write off any group of people, regardless of culture. He was not willing that any should perish, and that all should come to eternal life (2 Peter 3:9). In fact, the two miraculous feedings of Jesus, one of 5,000 people and another of 4,000, took place on opposite sides of the Sea of Galilee. The latter feeding was done on *the other side.* In both feedings, the Gospel writers tell us that there were remains; twelve baskets from the feeding of the 5,000 and seven baskets from the feeding of the 4,000. I believe that these exact numbers of leftovers have spiritual significance. The twelve baskets represent the twelve tribes of Israel, and the seven baskets signify the seven Canaanite nations (Deuteronomy 7:1) from which the people on *the other side* were descendants. Regardless of which side or what culture, Christ is the source of all blessing and life.

Jesus never neglected going to *the other side.* On one side of Galilee, the primary audience that Jesus ministered to was His own people. On *the other side* were those that can be compared with today's secular subculture of the bound and oppressed. My brother David once made an attempt to preach inside a New York City courtroom. It was, to say the least, not appreciated by those on the bench, but it was noticed by those on *the other side* of the law. After this ill-fated attempt, one of the gang members recognized David from the newspaper article and said to him, "Hey man, it looks like the cops don't like you either. You must be on our side."

That was a defining moment in David's effort to reach gangs. He was perceived to be on the side of the gangs. This was the opening of a new mission field and new ministry to an "unreached people group" of gangs and addicts. Hundreds of street missionaries would eventually follow and go through this open door to *the other side* that David Wilkerson had pioneered.

Going to *the other side* was a transition that required me to step outside the safety of the church walls where I felt secure, to the open air and the streets where I had to overcome fears and make cultural adjustments. I thought I knew what ministry was about. I thought that my training and upbringing had prepared me for the work I was called to do. But, I found that I had to learn the language and jargon of an entirely new culture that was as foreign to me as that of any distant country. I discovered that I needed to think in a new way about my calling into ministry as well as my personal relationship with my Lord. In the end, I found a whole new mission field of souls and lives that needed the kind of deliverance that only Jesus can bring. When Jesus and the others got to *the other side,* they found a man who wandered between death and despair with no one able to help him.

"*They came to the other side of the sea, into the country of Gerasenes. When He got out of the boat, immediately a man from the tombs with an unclean spirit met Him, and he had his dwelling among the tombs. And no one was able to bind him anymore, even with a chain; because he had often been bound with shackles and chains, and the chains had been torn apart by him and the shackles broken in pieces, and no one was strong enough to subdue him. Constantly, night and day, he was screaming among the tombs and in the mountains, and gashing himself with stones*" (Mark 5:1-5, NASB).

This "*man from the tombs*" was surrounded by death and bound by self-destructive behavior. He wandered from tomb to mountain, mutilating his body with sharp stones. Some of those on *the other side* to whom we are called to minister are also bound by the self-destructive behavior of drug addiction. Others may be bound by abusive family patterns or the idols of worldly prosperity and success. Wherever the agent, whatever the chains, those on *the other side* will remain bound in their conditions until someone gets into a boat and crosses over to minister to them.

Those people of *the other side* may be on *the other side* of the law or *the other side* of town or the other side of a divorce. Regardless, they hopelessly wander about, beyond the ability of a government agency or twelve-step program to change them, when changing is what they need. Some may find relief from symptoms for a while, but few will find true healing. They will not find healing for their lives until they find hope in their hearts to carry them beyond their own strength and struggles. There is only one cause and source of hope: Jesus Christ. And they will find Jesus through you as you answer your call to *the other side!*

> *How, then, can they call on the one they have not believed in? And how can they believe in the one of whom they have not heard? And how can they hear without someone preaching to them? And how can they preach unless they are sent? As it is written, 'How beautiful are the feet of those who bring good news!'* (Romans 10:14-15)

Often, we have no idea where God is taking us or what His purpose is when He gets us there. In his devotional, *My Utmost for His Highest*, Oswald Chambers speaks of the purpose of God and the perception of man:

> We are not taken into a conscious agreement with God's purpose. We are taken into God's purpose with no awareness of it at all. We have no idea what God's goal may be; as we continue, His purpose becomes even more and more vague. God's aim appears to have missed the mark, because we are too nearsighted to see the target at which He is aiming. At the beginning of the Christian life, we have our own ideas as to what God's purpose is. We say, 'God means for me to go over there,' and, 'God has

called me to do this special work.' We do what we think is right, and yet the compelling purpose of God remains upon us. The work we do is of no account when compared with the compelling purpose of God.[6]

The other side is that place of the "compelling purpose of God" as Oswald Chambers calls it. But, at the top of God's list is not anything that we will ever "do" for God, but rather that we walk closely behind Him in obedience, regardless of where He leads.

It took me several years to make the change mentally, spiritually and practically to the streets and street people, and then to provide the leadership for others to go to *the other side.* The Lord peeled off layer after layer of ego and expectation until He found a servant ready and willing to climb into the boat with Jesus and head off to that distant shore; we must be ready to be soft clay in the Potter's hands. Before we form our ministries, Christ will form His character in us, which is the basis of all ministries that we will ever do.

Directions to the Other Side

I don't know about you, but I require directions when I travel to a new place. Most directions are descriptions of what we will see on the way to our destination. Here are a few landmarks and truths that I have learned about *the other side.*

• *The other side* is the place where we minister out of our relationship with Christ, rather than our own experiences and expectations.

- *The other side* is the place where we must trust Christ for everything.
- *The other side* is the place where we are changed in the process of ministry.
- *The other side* is the place where we become fluent in a new language of love and grace.

A challenge lies before us as we climb into the boat to go to *the other side.* Be encouraged by the fact that there are people on that opposite shore who are waiting for our arrival. We hold the keys to their freedom and that of their families for generations yet unborn. We become the "Good News" to those who are perishing on *the other side.*

> *The Spirit of the Lord is on me, because he has anointed me to preach good news to the poor. He has sent me to proclaim freedom for the prisoners, and recovery of sight for the blind, to release the oppressed, to proclaim the year of the Lord's favor* (Luke 4:18-19).

(Note: This article is the first chapter from the book, *Going Over to the Other Side,* by Don Wilkerson.)[7]

29
WHY I LOVE THE CHURCH

I love your sanctuary, Lord, the place where your glorious presence dwells (Psalm 26:8).

I was glad when they said to me, "Let us go to the house of the LORD" (Psalm 122:1).

When I say I love the church, I speak of the organized body of believers who meet in a certain place and time. I have preached in churches of all types and sizes throughout the world. I've worshipped in denominational and non-denominational churches. I have ministered in mega-churches, small churches, and a church in Ethiopia with just a piece of canvas hanging over ropes. Wherever the church, the body of Christ meets, I love that place!

It pains me to see so many people turned off by the church; and others, believers, who have quit attending church, but still maintain their faith. Surveys show that about 19 percent of all who call themselves born-again Christians do not attend a local church on a regular basis. What sorrows me is that, in some cases, these complaints and issues with the church are valid. Yet, at the same time, I feel pain because I deeply love the church, and many of their complaints are not valid.

In a certain sense, we do not go to church, because we are the church. Our hearts, our lives are the dwelling place of God. So, wherever two or three are gathered together in Jesus' name, that constitutes the spiritual church. However, when I say I love the church, I am also talking about the organized, institutional church. Many make excuses for not attending a local church, saying they can love the Lord anywhere and without belonging to a church. I once asked a brother where his church was, and he replied, "Starbucks!" He was serious. He said that two other friends meet him there every Sunday morning for Bible study. At least their rent is cheap!

Some Christians also say they don't believe in denominations because they're too divisive, so they shun any church that belongs to a denomination. Yes, the divisions of the churches are harmful to the body of Christ, and denominationalism can become unhealthy, but we must not forget that denominations have reared up some of the greatest men and women of God.

I owe the church my life. I found my Savior through the church when I was eight years old. I can remember the minute details of the evening I accepted Jesus as a young lad. Though my parents were pastors, they never asked me whether I had accepted Jesus into my heart. I guess they assumed it. (If you have young children, never assume their salvation, just because they grew up in the church.) There comes a time and place for an open decision about Christ, and it can come at different ages depending on a child's understanding. I understood one evening when my parents took me to hear an evangelist friend of theirs preaching in another church. I was so proud to be with my parents because I was wearing a brand-new blue suit, and I thought I was a big deal. The adults were upstairs and children's church was downstairs. The evangelist's wife was speaking in children's church, and she gave an altar call and I accepted Jesus. The Gospel took root in my young heart.

Since then, I have seen the church at its best and at its worse, but I still love the church. I have seen church politics hurt my pastor/father, but I still love the church. I have been at times deeply hurt by church politics, but I still love the church. It was in church services where my call to the ministry was confirmed. I also have met some of the finest people on earth in church. I feel the presence of God in church services like no other place.

The world says the church is full of hypocrites, and yes, too many so-called Christians are a bad advertisement for the church. But non-members and non-attendees do not have the right to such complaints, for they do not see the other side. For every one hypocrite in the church, there are ten genuine followers of Christ.

The hypocrite's excuse of not attending church holds no water. *"The Church is not a gallery for exhibition of eminent Christians, but a school for the education of the imperfect ones"* (Henry Ward Beecher).[1] If the main thing the church can be accused of is having hypocrites attending it, then the church is in good shape.

Eugene Peterson writes about hypocrisy in his Introduction to the Epistle of James in the Message Bible:

> *When Christian believers gather in churches, everything that can go wrong sooner or later does. Outsiders, on observing this, conclude that there is nothing in the religion business except, perhaps business—and dishonest business at that. Insiders see it differently. Just as a hospital collects the sick under one roof and labels*

them as such, the church collects sinners. Many of the people outside the hospital are every bit as sick as the ones inside, but their illnesses are either undiagnosed or disguised. It's similar with sinners outside the church. So Christian churches are not, as a rule, model communities of good behavior. They are, rather, places where human misbehavior is brought out in the open, faced, and dealt with.[2]

The only ones, in my estimation, that have the right to complain about the church are those who are faithful to a church. It is because we love the church so much that we point out its flaws. We want to see the church change. (By the way, if you're one who complains that the church is full of hypocrites, come on in. We've got room for one more.) Yet, with all the problems a church may have, it is God's instrument to reach the world for Jesus Christ. The church has many critics, but no rivals.

I am fortunate to have seen the church from a national and international perspective. Yes, there are dead churches. There is dull preaching and traditional worship that can put you right to sleep. But one church does not define the body of Christ.

The church we love [may be] as flawed and messed up as we are, but [the church is in fact] Christ's bride, nonetheless. And I may as well have a basement without a house or a head without a body as despise the wife my Savior loves (Kevin DeYoung).[3]

There is a phenomenon today that was not seen decades ago; that is, people who find their spiritual growth outside the local church. They may belong to a small, independent cell group (today's version of the New Testament house church). They may follow some well-known teacher; or as one man told me, "My pastor feeds me spiritually on CDs, DVDs and the Ipad." Even Billy Graham recognized this, saying, *"Unless the church quickly recovers the authoritative, biblical message, we may witness the spectacle of millions of Christians going outside the institutional church to find spiritual food."*

While recognizing the truth of Graham's statement, I say it's time to state what is right with the church. Let me share a few things with you as to what I feel is right with the church, looking at the entire body of Christ worldwide.

1. The Church will always be constant, and it will withstand any and all attacks against it.

Jesus declared, *"I will build my church, and the gates of Hades will not overcome it"* (Matthew 16:18). It may be crude to say so, but good, bad or indifferent the church will still be here tomorrow in some form until Jesus comes. I have met some mean-spirited people in the church, as well. In one church, some deacons were giving my Dad trouble and there was a board meeting scheduled to take place—and apparently it was not going to be a pastor-friendly meeting. My brother David heard about it and snuck in the basement of the church—with a baseball bat. If necessary, he was going to defend my pastor father. He was just a lad, I might add.

I am not here to defend the church of Jesus Christ. It has, it is, and it always will continue to stand on the foundation of Jesus Christ. *"The Church of Jesus Christ is built on these two things: The divine revelation of who Jesus is, and the public confession of it"* (Oswald Chambers).[4] That's what Jesus meant when He told Peter that, *"Upon this rock I will build My church."* Peter had just given his confession of faith when Jesus said this. Jesus said, *"And the rain descended, and the floods came, and the winds blew, and beat upon the house and it fell not: for it was founded upon a rock"* (Matthew 7:25).

> *The church always seems behind the times, when it is really beyond the times; it is waiting till the last fad shall have seen its last summer. It keeps the key to permanent virtue* (G. K. Chesterton).[5]

Chesterton said, in effect, that the Rotary Club might dissolve, "...but when we belong to the Church, we belong to something which is outside all of us; which is outside everything you talk about, outside."

Years ago, there was a Baptist church in Georgia. (The small town may have been called Goose Creek, but I am not sure). What I am sure of is that the pastor wanted to build a new church in the center of the village on an empty lot. The owner lived next door to the lot, so the pastor asked if the man had plans to build on the lot and he said, "No."

"Will you sell us the lot?" The owner said, "No."

The pastor kept asking and every time the lot owner refused to sell.

One night a flash flood hit the village and some deacons of the church looked out to see that the church was floating down the road. They gathered some men, tied ropes around the church to guide it straight down the road as it seemed the church was going to float to the other side of the village. As they did so, the floating church made a right hand turn as if it had a will of its own. Then the church made a left hand turn and stopped and settled on the very lot the pastor tried to purchase.

The next morning the pastor got a knock on his door. It was the lot owner. He handed the pastor the deed to his lot and said, "You win."

The church of Jesus Christ down through the ages has endured floods of false teachings, false prophets, and false profits. It has endured attacks from governments, courts, dictators, communism, other 'isms" and still the church stands. Yes, the church is weak in some places, strong in other places—but it stands. The church will always win, because Christ is the Head.

2. I love the Church because it's the place where light is separated from the darkness.

I realize that we are to be the light of the world, but I need the church to rekindle the fire in my soul so I can be that light. Growing up in Sunday School, we used to sing "This little light of mine, I'm gonna let it shine." One verse says, "Don't let Satan blow it out." It is one of Satan's main goals to blow out the light of the saints. When I come into the church, for me the world is shut out and I am shut in with Christ—the Light of my salvation.

Paul wrote in 2 Timothy a list of deeds done in the darkness—this is some list! *"There will be terrible times in the last days. People will be lovers of themselves, lovers of money, boastful, proud, abusive, disobedient to their parents, ungrateful, unholy, without love, unforgiving, slanderous, without self-control, brutal, not lovers of the good, treacherous, rash, conceited, lovers of pleasure rather than lovers of God—having a form of godliness but denying its power. Have nothing to do with them."* The KJV says, *"From such turn away."* We are to have nothing to do with participating in the deeds of those in darkness. Yes, we are to win such people to Christ, but if you are constantly surrounded by darkness, it can wear on you and weary you.

For me, the church is the equivalent to the miracle of the ninth plague in Egypt. Exodus 10:21 says, *"Total darkness covered all Egypt for three days...Yet all the Israelites had light in the places where they lived."*

I have been doing a personal study in the Book of Psalms and I noticed something I never saw before. I have been discovering the importance of the church in the Psalms. Again and again, when the writers talked about being surrounded by evil and evil doers, they sought refuge in the house of God and with the people of God. Here are a few examples: *"My soul is among lions...whose teeth are spears and arrows, and their tongue a sharp sword"* (Psalm 57:4). What did the Psalmist then do? *"I will praise you, O Lord, among the people"* (Verse 9). I have always loved Psalm 27:4: *"One thing have I desired of the Lord, that will I seek after; that I may dwell in the house of the Lord all the days of my life, to behold the beauty of the Lord, and to inquire in his temple."*

However, what I failed to see is the context in which David wrote this. In the same chapter he talks about his enemies and foes who wanted to destroy him. David always spoke of having *"a host encamp against him."* At such a time David sought comfort, encouragement and strength by offering sacrifices of joy in God's house.

I am somewhat of a news junkie, at times buying three newspapers a day and subscribing to four national news magazines monthly. My wife says, "Why do you read all this." I tell her this is why I am so smart. She says, "You sure got me fooled." If I listen to too much local, national or international news, I can find myself thinking politically or carnally and I then need to separate myself from the darkness for a while and get shut in with God. But I need something more than my personal time with the Lord. I need to be with the family of God and worship corporately. I need a word from the pulpit.

2 Corinthians 4:6 says, *"For God, who said, "Let light shine out of darkness" made His light to shine in our hearts to give us the light of the knowledge of the glory of God in the face of Jesus Christ."* This Light eclipses the darkness in which we are surrounded.

3. The Church for me is a place I go to for a drink at Joel's Bar.

I'm an avid book reader and one of the books I have is entitled, *A Drink at Joel's Bar.* The title is based on the Old Testament Book of Joel that says *"It shall come to pass afterward, that I will pour out my spirit upon all flesh"* (2:28). This was fulfilled on the day of Pentecost, and continues to be fulfilled in church gatherings to all who are thirsty.

I need the church because the work of the ministry can be very draining, both of my physical and spiritual energy. I have come back from speaking tours overseas totally, physically drained, and I'd force myself to get to the house of God; not to preach, but to soak—to soak in the presence of God. There is something about corporate praise and worship that is spiritually and physically energizing. Psalm 63:1-3 says, *"O God you are my God; I earnestly search for you. My soul thirsts for you; my whole body longs for you in this parched and weary land where there is no water. I have seen you in your sanctuary and gazed upon your power and glory."*

I find that some ministry workers and ministers come under undeserved condemnation, when they are simply spiritually dry. Some attribute this dryness to a lack of love for Christ when, in fact, it's the result of pouring out His love to the lost and needy. This dryness needs to drive us to Joel's Bar when one can taste and see that the Lord is good.

Are you spiritually dry—spiritually parched and feeling condemned for it? Perhaps you're attributing the spiritual dryness to the wrong thing. We have this treasure in earthen vessels, which means that the outer man can be drained, exhausted, worn out mentally and emotionally. There's nothing wrong with you. You just need a drink from Joel's Bar. Many times the Holy Spirit is being poured out in our midst, but we're not receiving because we're too focused on analyzing ourselves. Or worse, we're having a pity party, blaming it all on the devil, giving him credit for something he does not deserve.

An old worship chorus we used to sing says, "Fill my cup Lord, I lift it up Lord—come and quench this thirsting of my soul." Paul commanded, *"Quench not the Spirit"* (1 Thessalonians 5:19). The church is a filling station, a refueling place.

A woman woke her husband up on a Sunday morning and said, "Honey, it's time to get up and get ready for church."

He said, "I don't wanna go! Why do I have to go to church?"

His wife said, "You have to go to church because you're the pastor."

I've had times like that, when I had to drag myself to church. I went in weak, and came out strong! I went to church down, and came out high in the Spirit. Psalm 36:8 declares, *"They feast on the abundance of your house, and you give them drink from the river of your delights."* D.L. Moody wrote, *"You may as well try to hear without ears, or breathe without lungs, as try to live a Christian life without the Spirit of God in your heart."* Happy hour is not at the local tavern or bar—happy hour is in the house of God.

4. I love the Church because it's where we find healing when and if a Church has done us wrong.

If you go to a doctor and he does a procedure that turns out to be wrong, do you go to a garage mechanic to correct the procedure? In an imperfect church there are believers who have been hurt or wounded by church members. Maybe you're one of them! Zechariah 13:6 says, *"If someone asks, 'What are these wounds in your body?' He will answer, The wounds I was given at the house of my friends.'"* Unfortunately, there are churches that have wounded people spiritually and emotionally, and this is a fact that can't be denied. Ironically, it is in the church where you can be healed from hurts or wounds inflicted by someone in the body of Christ.

I think of a young lady who is 29 years old. She was raised in the church until she was 12. One Sunday her mother got upset with the pastor. She left the church for good and took her daughter with her and never went back to any church. This young girl as a result ended up becoming addicted to drugs, and eventually was diagnosed as being mentally unbalanced and suicidal. She then became a cutter, slashing her body to harm herself. The list of her problems goes on and on. It all started when she left the church, although it was no fault of her own. Thankfully, she ended up in a Teen Challenge program, graduated, and is now my Executive Assistant; and she's on fire for God!

If your physical body gets an infection, there are cells in your body that will attack the disease and contribute to the body's healing. As in the natural body, so in the spiritual body!

When I was sixteen years old, I went to my pastor father's denominational conference where he was fully expected to be elected to a District Executive position. He was utterly crushed when he was not elected. The reason he was voted down was because he took a stand publicly against immorality of another church leader in the denomination. That man politicked against my father, so my father did not get the votes he expected. My father was never the same after this—and I watched all this up close and personal, just as I was about to study for the ministry. Thankfully, this never embittered me. I still loved the church, in spite of what happened to my father.

If you have been hurt in or by a church, your healing can come through the church. I'm not saying the church itself will heal you—Christ is our Healer. But He does His work of healing through the body of Christ, the church.

30
WHAT TEEN CHALLENGE
CAN TEACH THE CHURCH

Teen Challenge is a place that we can call, *The Land of Beginning Again.* I take this title from a poem by Louis Fletcher of which I quote now a few verses:

I wish that there were some wonderful place,
called the Land of Beginning Again,
Where all our mistakes and all our heartaches
and all of our selfish grief
Could be dropped like a shabby old coat at the door
and never put on again.[1]

I would like to share with you how Teen Challenge can be a blessing and encouragement to the church in at least four ways:

1. We are a ministry that sees the fulfillment of Romans 5:20, *"Where sin abounds grace doth much more abound"* (KJV).

In all my years working in Teen Challenge, I have never had to convince one of our residents that they are sinners. All of our residents have a past they are not proud of and want to forget. But one thing is sure: regardless of one's past record, their sin and sins can be forgiven because of the grace of God.

2. At Teen Challenge, we see visible evidence of the fact that God's arm has a long, long reach. Isaiah 50:2 says, *"Is my arm shortened, that it cannot save?"*

Some of these students have known what is often called the long arm of the law. Now they have known the long arm of God to reach them and lift them from the depths of despair—setting them free from every bondage. God can pull a man out of the bar room. He can pull an addict out of a dope house. Christ can pull a criminal out of physical, mental, and emotional prisons. God's arm is not afraid to reach way down into a mud pit and save a rebel, a backslider, or reach way up to a proud man or woman who thinks they are above the need for God. I love to see the reach of God's love that takes a broken heart and heals it; takes a broken marriage and saves it; takes a prodigal and returns him or her to the Father's house.

3. Jesus Christ is the cure!

In Teen Challenge we believe that according to 2 Corinthians 5:17, *"If any man [or woman] be in Christ, old things pass away; behold, all things become new."* When you are born again, the old habits and addictions die, and a new person is resurrected in and with Christ.

4. Teen Challenge can inspire hope for all who are praying for an unsaved loved one; and especially if that loved one has a serious life-controlling problem.

As Teen Challenge students and graduates share their testimonies, it fosters faith in the hearer's heart that God can (and will) do the same miraculous, merciful intervention in the lives of those we are praying for.

END NOTES

Chapter 1: The Slothfulness of Busyness
1. Phileena Heuertz, *Pilgrimage of a Soul* (Downers Grove: IVP Books, 2010), 26-27.
2. Andy Stanley, *Next Generation Leader* (Colorado Springs: Multnomah Books, 2006), 34.
3. J. C. Ryle, *The Upper Room: Being a Few Truths for the Times*, www.ccel.org/ccel/ryle/upper_room.txt
4. Brother Lawrence, *Practicing the Presence of God* (Grand Rapids: Revell, 1967), 14.
5. Charles Swindoll, *So You Want To Be Like Christ?* (Nashville: Thomas Nelson, 2005), 9.

Chapter 2: Front Sliding
1. A. W. Tozer, *The A. W. Tozer Bible* (Peabody: Hendrickson Publishers, 2012), 1186.

Chapter 3: How to Stay Faithful in a Thankless Environment
1. Damian Kyle, *Unappreciated: Serving God in a Thankless Environment* http://www.calvarychapelmodesto.com
2. James Richards, *The Complete Guide to Christian Quotations* (Uhrichsville: Barbour Publishing, 2011), 100.
3. Ibid.

Chapter 4: What Can Eldad and Medad Teach Us Today?
1. Luis Palau, *Heart After God* (Portland: Multnomah, 1982), 35.
2. Henry Drummond, *The Greatest Thing In The World* (New York: Fleming H. Revell, 1981), 16.
3. Http://davidwilkersontoday.blogspot.com/2009/09/seeds-of-jealousy-and-envy.html

Chapter 6. Signs and Wonders
1. Henry Drummond, quoted in Bruce Bickel, Stan Jantz, *Knowing the Bible 101* (Eugene: Harvest House Publishers, 1998), 209.
2. Augustine, quoted in Blaise Pascal, *Thoughts* (New York: P.F. Collier & Son, 1909), 216.
3. Katherine Kuhlman, quoted in *The Complete Guide to Christian Quotations* (Uhrichsville: Barbour Publishing, 2011), 279.
4. W. Galloway Tyson, quoted in Daniel Whyte, III, *Letters to Young Black Women* (Joshua: Torch Legacy Publications, 2006), 106.
5. Steve Sampson, quoted in *The Complete Guide to Christian Quotations* (Uhrichsville: Barbour Publishing, 2011), 279.

6. Matthew Arnold, *The Works of Matthew Arnold* (Charleston: Nabu Press, 2010), 128.

7. Tim Keller, *The Reason for God* (New York: Penguin Group, 2008), 86.

8. Charles Haddon Spurgeon, *Metropolitan Tabernacle Pulpit: Volume 38* (Carlisle: Banner of Truth, 1987), 26.

Chapter 7. Para-Christians

1. Don Wilkerson, *Within a Yard of Hell* (Brewster: Paraclete Press, 1987), 147.

2. Bill Hybels, *Just Walk Across the Room* (Grand Rapids: Zondervan, 2006), 45.

Chapter 8. Authority

1. Samuel Smiles, quoted in *The Speaker's Quote Book by Roy B. Zuck* (Grand Rapids: Kregel Publications, 1997), 29.

2. Anne Bradstreet, *The Poems of Mrs. Anne Bradstreet,* compiled by Frank Easton (Kila: Kessinger Publishing, 2010), 12.

3. Catherine Marshall, *Beyond Our Selves* (Ada: Chosen Books, 2001), 194.

Chapter 9. Spiritual Gift Mix

1. J. E. O' Day, *Discovering Your Spiritual Gifts* (Downers Grove: InterVarsity Press, 1985), 3.

2. I. Howard Marshall, *1 Peter New Testament Commentary* (Downers Grove: InterVarsity Press, 1991), 146.

3. Charles Hodge, *1 Corinthians* (Wheaton: Crossway, 1995), 213.

Chapter 10. The Untitled Leader

1. Mark Sanborn, *You Don't Need a Title to Be a Leader* (New York: Crown Business, 2006), ii.

2. John Maxwell, *Becoming a Person of Influence* (Nashville: Thomas Nelson, 1997), 3.

3. John Maxwell, *Leadership Promises for Everyday* (Nashville: Thomas Nelson, 2007), July 27th entry.

4. Jill Briscoe, *A Little Pot of Oil* (Sisters: Multnomah Publishers, 2003), 8.

Chapter 11. Everyone Needs an "And"

1. A. W. Tozer, *The Reaper,* Feb. 1962, pp. 459.

1. A. W. Tozer, *Success and the Christian* (Camp Hill: Christian Publications, 1994), 86.

Chapter 12. The "Other Curriculum

1. Albert Schweitzer, quoted in *Developing the Leaders Around You* by John C. Maxwell (Nashville: Thomas Nelson, 1995), 20.
2. Rick Renner, *Sparkling Gems* (Tulsa: Teach All Nations, 2003), Jan. 16.
3. Ibid.
4. W. M. Lewis, quoted in *Sacred Simplicities: Meeting the Miracles in Our Lives* by Lori Knutson (Toronto: Dundurn, 2004), 33.

Chapter 14. Staying Out Front

1. Robert E. Lee, *Jokes Quotes & Anecdotes* by A. Daniel Goldsmith (www.xulonpress.com, 2010), 96.
2. Charles H. Spurgeon, *Spurgeon's Sermons on the Cross of Christ* (Grand Rapids: Kregel, 1993), 51.

Chapter 15. The Use & Misuse of Information

1. Roy B. Zuck, *The Speaker's Quotebook* (Grand Rapids : Kregel Publications, 1997), 230.
2. Beth Moore, *Breaking Free, Updated Edition* (Nashville: B&H Publishing Group, 2009), 15.
3. Croft M. Pentz, *1001 Things Your Mother Told You and You Have Listened To!* (Carol Stream: Tyndale House Publishers, 2001), 161.

Chapter 16. Waffling On No

1. Matthew Henry, *Commentary on the Whole Bible,* (Peabody: Hendrickson Publishers, 2008), Commentary on Genesis, Chapter 3.
2. A. W. Tozer, *Fellowship of the Burning Heart* (Accessible Publishing Systems PTY Ltd., 2010)
3. Source unknown.

Chapter 17. Lessons from Ittai and Shimei

1. Kay Arthur, *When Bad Things Happen* (Colorado Springs: Waterbrook Press, 2000), 91.

Chapter 18. No Sweat

1. David Platt, *Radical* (Colorado Springs: Multnomah Books, 2010), Chapter 3.
2. E.M. Bounds, *Power Through Prayer* (Grand Rapids: Zondervan Publishing House, 1962), 18.
3. Charles Spurgeon, quotes in *http://simple.wikiquote.org/wiki/Charles_Spurgeon*

Chapter 19. Calling and Enabling

1. Billy Graham, quoted in *Billy Graham in Quotes* by Franklin Graham (Nashville: Thomas Nelson, 2011), 308.

2. J. E. O' Day, *Discovering Your Spiritual Gifts* (Downers Grove: InterVarsity Press, 1985), 6.

3. John Mason, *An Enemy Called Average* (Tulsa: Insight Publishing Group, 1990), 18.

Chapter 20. Listening

1. Larry King, Quoted in *The Little Red Book of Wisdom,* (Nashville, Thomas Nelson, 2011), 149.

2. Peter Drucker, quoted in *Shut Up and Say Something,* by Karen Friedman (Westport: Praeger, 2010), 165.

3. Bruce Brickel and Stan Jantz, *God is in the Small Stuff* (Uhrichsville: Barbour Publishing, 1998), Chapter 24.

4. Epictetus, quoted in *A Quote For Every Day,* by Peter A. LaPorta (Bloomington: AuthorHouse, 2011), 317.

5. George Dana Boardman. Quotes.net, STANDS4 LLC, 2012. http://www.quotes.net/quote/10981, accessed September 7, 2012.

6. Paul Tillich, quoted in *Beyond Maintenance to Mission: A Theology of the Congregation* by Craig L. Nessan (Minneapolis: Fortress Press, 2010), 15.

7. Dietrich Bonhoeffer, *Life Together* (New York: Harper & Brothers, 1959), 18.

8. John C. Maxwell, *Everyone Communicates, Few Connect* (Nashville: Thomas Nelson, 2010), 187.

9. H. Norman Wright, *Helping Those Who Hurt* (Bloomington: Bethany House Publishers, 2006), 40.

Chapter 21. Cheap Education

1. C. H. Spurgeon, quoted in *Entrusted with the Gospel: Pastoral Expositions of 2 Timothy* edited by D. A. Carson (Wheaton: Crossway, 2010), 139.

2. William Cunningham, quoted in *The Speaker's Quote Book* by Roy B. Zuck (Grand Rapids: Kregel, 1997), 163.

3. Peter Drecker, quoted in *The Speaker's Quote Book* by Roy B. Zuck (Grand Rapids: Kregel Publications, 1997), 161.

4. Ralph Waldo Emerson, quoted in *Teaching With Care,* edited by Lenore Sandel (Newark: International Reading Association, 2006), 20.

5. William James. Thinking Thoughts, 2012. http://www.tboleware.com/, accessed September 7, 2012.

6. Mark Twain, *The Wit and Wisdom of Mark Twain,* by Alex Ayres (New York: Harper Perennial, 2005), 66.

7. Robert Fulghum, *All I Really Need to Know I Learned in Kindergarten,* (New York: Ballantine, 2004), 1.

8. Keith Anderson, *Spiritual Mentoring,* (Downers Grove: IVP Books, 1999)

9. Ted Engstrom, *The Making of a Mentor*, (Waynesboro: Authentic Press, 2005)

Chapter 22. Most of My Mentors are Dead

1. John Piper, Brothers, *We Are Not Professionals,* (Nashville: Broadman & Holman Publishers, 2002), 89.

2. Jules Renard, quoted in *The Greatest Quotations of All-Time* by Anthony St. Peter (Bloomington: Xlibris, 2010), 336.

3. C. T. Studd, *C. T. Studd: No Retreat* by Janet Benge (Seattle: YWAM Publishing 2005), 150.

4. Hudson Taylor, quoted in *Living for Christ* by Christin Ditchfield (Ventura: Gospel Light, 2011), 35.

5. C. H. Spurgeon, *Lectures to My Students* (Charleston: Nabu Press, 2010), 72.

6. Charles "Tremendous" Jones, quoted in *Know Your Limits-Then Ignore Them by John Mason* (Tulsa: Insight Publishing Group, 1999)

7. Peter Lillback, *George Washington's Sacred Fire* (King of Prussia: Providence Forum Press, 2006)

8. A. W. Tozer, *A. W. Tozer: A Twentieth Century Prophet* (Camp Hill: Christian Publications, 1964), 149.

9. Croft M. Pentz, *1001 Things Your Mother Told You and You Have Listened To!* (Carol Stream: Tyndale House Publishers, 2001), 84.

Chapter 23. Beware of the Presumption of Friendships

1. Robert Louis Stevenson, quoted in *The Speaker's Quote Book* by Roy B. Zuck (Grand Rapids: Kregel Publications, 1997), 206.

2. Mark Twain, quoted in *The Oxford Dictionary of American Quotations* by Hugh Rawson and Margaret Miner (New York: Oxford University Press, 2005), 279.

3. Francis de Sales. Daily with de Sales. http://www.oblates.org/dss/daily_with_desales/, accessed September 7, 2012.

4. Charles Swindoll, *Swindoll's Ultimate Book of Illustrations & Quotes,* (Nashville: Thomas Nelson, 2003)

5. Ralph Waldo Emerson, quoted in *Wiersbe Bible Commentary NT*, by Warren W. Wiersbe (Colorado Springs: David C. Cook, 2007), 379.

6. Howard and William Hendricks, *As Iron Sharpens Iron* (Chicago: Moody Publishers, 1999)

7. Lilian Whiting, quoted in *The Speaker's Quote Book by Roy B. Zuck* (Grand Rapids: Kregel Publications, 1997)

8. Traci Mullins, *Celebrating Friendship* (Grand Rapids: Zondervan Publishing House, 1998)

9. Croft M. Pentz, *1001 Things Your Mother Told You and You Have Listened To!* (Carol Stream: Tyndale House Publishers, 2001)

Chapter 24. The Shrinking Pulpit

1. Charles Swindoll, *Swindoll's Ultimate Book of Illustrations & Quotes* (Nashville: Thomas Nelson, 2003)

2. John Piper, *Brothers We Are Not Professionals* (Nashville: Broadman & Holman Publishers, 2002)

3. Vance Havner, *Journey from Jugtown*, by Douglas Malcolm White (New York: F. H. Revell, 1977), 137.

4. C. H. Spurgeon, *Spurgeon at His Best* (Ada: Baker, 1988), 61.

5. Chuck Colson, *The Oprahfication of Religion*, http://luke418min.com/page75.html

6. C. H. Spurgeon, *Spurgeon at His Best* (Ada: Baker, 1988), 85.

Chapter 25. How to Play Second Fiddle

1. Martin Luther, quoted in *1 Corinthians: A Shorter Exegetical and Pastoral Commentary* by Anthony C. Thiselton (Grand Rapids: Eerdmans, 2011), 98.

2. Beth Moore, *A Beautiful Mind, Teaching Series*, 1999

3. Quoted by John C. Maxwell, *The 360 Degree Leader,* (Nashville: Thomas Nelson, 2005)

Chapter 27. The Trans-Generational Church

1. Quoted in *Special Sermons* by George Sweeting (Chicago: Moody Press. 1985), 90.

2. Billy Graham, *Till Armageddon* (Nashville: Thomas Nelson, 1984), 62.

3. Lyman Bryson, *1001 Quotes, Illustrations, and Humorous Stories* (Ada: Baker Books, 2008)

4. Jeff Leeland, *Disarming the Teenage Heart* (Sharon: Life Journey, 2003)

5. George MacDonald, quoted in Good Quotes, http://www.goodquotes.com/quote/george-macdonald/when-we-are-out-of-sympathy-with-the-y

Chapter 28. Called to the Other Side

1. Don Wilkerson, *Called to the Other Side,* Teen Challenge International (2002)

2. Oswald Chambers, *My Utmost For His Highest,* August 3rd reading, utmost.org/the-compelling-purpose-of-god/

Chapter 29. Why I Love the Church

1. Henry Ward Beecher, quoted in Making Disciples, by (Maitland: Xulon Press, 2012), 84.

2. Eugene Peterson, The Message (Colorado Springs: NavPress, 2002) Introduction to the Epistle of James.

3. Kevin DeYoung, Why We Love the Church (Chicago: Moody, 2009)

4. Oswald Chambers, Bringing Sons into Glory (Marshall, Morgan & Scott, 1958)

5. G. K. Chesterton, The Wit and Wisdom of G. K. Chesterton (New York: Continuum, 2011)

Chapter 30. What Teen Challenge Can Teach the Church

1. The Louise Fletcher poem, *"The Land of Beginning Again,"* was found in the notes of Dr. Herbert C. Gabhart, President of Belmont University (1959-1982), in the archives at Belmont University.

.

Also by Don Wilkerson

"It's full of wisdom, bringing the God-factor to the forefront as The Remedy to the problem. The author has spent 54 years working with Teen Challenge, helping to rehabilitate thousands of addicts. He knows firsthand what works."
-Jesse Owens-President, Global Renewal, Inc.

"To read this book is like chatting with him (Pastor Don Wilkerson) over a good hot meal, where he'll tell you the truth, with genuine fatherly love."
-Pastor Charles Simpson, Oasis Christian Center, LIC, NY

"I purposely wrote YOUR FIRST STEP TO FREEDOM for those who know in their heart of hearts they need help, but have, thus far, been unwilling to do anything about it. Perhaps they are too proud, too fearful, or have never heard that they can be free of their problem by raising their hands to God and asking for his supernatural help."
-Pastor Don
Wilkerson Co-Founder of Teen Challenge
and Times Square Church

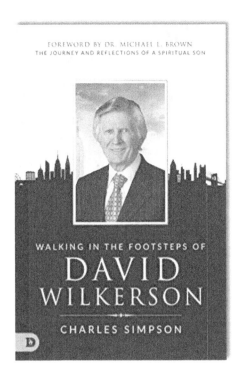

David Wilkerson was a true general of the faith, recognized for his world-impacting ministries Teen Challenge, World Challenge, and Times Square Church, as well as his bestselling book, The Cross and the Switchblade. He was known worldwide for his fiery passion for evangelism. During his 80 years on earth, Wilkerson brought the love of God to gangs and drug dealers, helping countless individuals defeat the giants of addiction, violence, and torment.

David Wilkerson impacted many lives for eternity but some were close enough to him to walk in his footsteps. Charles Simpson was one of these. In WALKING IN THE FOOTSTEPS OF DAVID WILKERSON, Charles Simpson shares his experiences, as well as the deep revelations he received under Wilkerson's leadership. Today, David Wilkerson's example is your invitation to be used by God in supernatural ways.

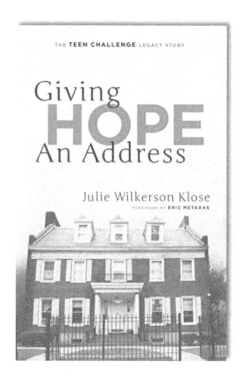

Two Brothers, One Calling, and a Lasting Legacy. For sixty years, the faith-based ministry of Teen Challenge has been bringing hope to those bound by drug and life-controlling addictions. Since the very first Teen Challenge Center opened its doors in Brooklyn, New York the ministry has grown to 1,400 Centers across 122 nations. This faith story exemplifies what it means to be a follower of Christ; to love the broken-hearted and share the gospel of Jesus Christ bringing light into the darkness (John 12:46).

GIVING HOPE AN ADDRESS reveals how God's calling on the lives of two brothers leads to many other life-changing stories. The spiritual battle against addiction can still be won. This story of Teen Challenge and its legacy proves it.

The Mission of Teen Challenge

Teen Challenge is a Christian-based organization. The purpose of TC is to help people who have life-controlling problems and initiate the discipleship process to the point where the student can function as a Christian in society. The TC approach is to teach a whole new way of living by addressing family relationships, work attitudes, self-image and esteem, peer pressure, addictions, social issues, community relationship, and a variety of other life skills. Teen Challenge endeavors to help people become mentally sound, emotionally balanced, socially adjusted, physically well, and spiritually alive. Teen Challenge is the oldest, largest and most successful program of its kind in the world.

Brooklyn Teen Challenge

Based in Brooklyn, Teen Challenge works with adults whose lives have been impacted by drug addiction and other serious life-controlling problems. The core services of the ministry are the 12-18 month holistic residential recovery program for men and women. Don Wilkerson, the original Co-Founder, is the Director of Brooklyn Teen Challenge.

Brooklyn Teen Challenge
444 Clinton Avenue
Brooklyn, NY 11238
(718) 789-1414

www.brooklyntc.org

Made in United States
North Haven, CT
07 February 2023

32184710R00104